THE
Discipline
Miracle

THE
Clinically Proven System
for Raising Happy, Healthy,
and Well-Behaved Kids

Dr. Linda Pearson,
DNSc, Family Psychiatric Mental Health Nurse Practitioner
WITH L.A. Stamford

AMACOM
AMERICAN MANAGEMENT ASSOCIATION
New York | Atlanta | Brussels | Chicago | Mexico City
San Francisco | Shanghai | Tokyo | Washington D.C.

This publication is designed to provide accurate and authoritative information in regard to the subject matter covered. It is sold with the understanding that the publisher is not engaged in rendering legal, accounting, or other professional service. If legal advice or other expert assistance is required, the services of a competent professional person should be sought.

Library of Congress Cataloging-in-Publication Data

Pearson, Linda Joan.
    The discipline miracle : the clinically proven system for raising happy, healthy, and well-behaved kids / Linda Pearson.
        p. cm.
    Includes index.
    ISBN 0-8144-7297-4
    1. Discipline of children.   2. Child rearing.   I. Title.
    HQ770.4.P43   2006
    649'.64—dc22   2005021052

Printing number

10 9 8 7 6 5 4 3 2 1

Contents

CHAPTER 1

Kids and Problem Behaviors

It's likely that the reason you picked up this book is because things don't always go perfectly with your child. In fact, sometimes they go horribly wrong. You're wondering if these difficulties are huge or just bumps in the road. But, in either case, your child's problem behaviors are making things a lot tougher than you think they should be, and you need to find an effective way to deal with them.

Do you sometimes feel as if you are on a "wheel of emotions" with your child? He does something that angers or frustrates you. Then you become angry at yourself for being angry at him, and now you feel even angrier at him because he was able to make you so angry with yourself. And, when he does the same thing just after you yelled at him to stop, you feel even angrier than you did a few minutes before. Does your child have an incredible ability to trigger emotions you didn't even know you had until he was born?

I feel confident that after reading this book you will have a new perspective on how to approach your parenting challenges.

Parenting is a tough job. Raising toddlers and preschoolers is filled with ever-changing problem behaviors that you can expect to experience. Trust me when I say that whatever you're going through, you are not alone. And this is a good thing. Because you can benefit from my experience and the experience of all of the people I've worked with over the years.

Do any of these situations sound familiar?

❏ **EIGHTEEN-MONTH-OLD LINDA WHINES,** clings to her mom Yvette's legs, and always wants to be held. Yvette tries to give her all the love she has, but sometimes she tries to detach herself to get other things done. Then, she feels guilty and wonders if she is doing the right thing.

❏ **TWO-AND-A-HALF-YEAR-OLD THOMAS** is a strong-willed child who constantly demands his own way and seems to draw a great deal of power from saying NO to any request from his mother and father. His parents often feel helpless and tired from the stress of dealing with their first born. Sometimes they even feel a secret desire to escape from the responsibilities of raising him.

❏ **THREE-AND-A-HALF-YEAR-OLD LENNY** whines all the time. His mom Carolyn tells him repeatedly to stop, each time becoming more and more frustrated. By the third time, she raises her voice in an attempt to get his attention. Still, Lenny continues whining and pleading. She ends up screaming at him, and this stops him temporarily. But now Carolyn feels guilty and resents that becoming angry seems to be the only approach that works.

❏ **FOUR-AND-A-HALF-YEAR-OLD CHRIS** has an activity level that won't quit. He never seems to listen, and he won't sit still for anything other than action shows on television. Chris also has trouble changing what he is doing. If he is playing in the house, he doesn't want to leave for the playground. And once there, he creates a scene when his dad John needs to take him home again. Sometimes John just leaves him in front of the television for hours, even though he feels guilty doing this. He often just lacks the energy to "fight with him" and feels exhausted as a parent.

❏ **FIVE-AND-A-HALF-YEAR-OLD AMY** hates the feeling of tags or rough clothing—and she positively won't eat anything that is the least bit cold or hot or "looks funny." Amy's mom Donna feels as if she is raising a princess who demands that everything be done her way even though this still doesn't make Amy happy. In Donna's mind, everything she has tried so far has failed. She has no idea what to do next.

If any of these scenarios ring a bell—and this is just the tip of the iceberg—the suggestions in this book should help you.

Whether your child's problem behaviors are big or small, whether they indicate a stage he is going through or something far more serious, you can take steps that will make a lifelong difference for you both. And throughout the course of this book, you will learn those steps, as well as how to use them and customize them to your particular situation.

But before we begin, let's come to an understanding about what problem behaviors are and where they come from.

What are Problem Behaviors?

Problem behaviors can be defined in many ways. A child's behavior is a problem if it causes a parent to feel unpleasant emotions (such as anger, bewilderment, disappointment, or guilt). It's a problem if it causes the child to act in a way that regularly upsets others.

It's a problem if a child seems to be unhappy, anxious, or angry a lot of the time. And it's a problem if it gets in the way of his getting along with others.

If your child regularly exhibits any of these behaviors, does that mean that she is "sick"? Not at all! A certain amount of misbehavior in your tot and preschooler is perfectly normal. There is no such thing as continuous peace with our youngsters. Parents who think that their lives *should* be calm when their children are this age are often terribly disappointed and are setting themselves up for a fall.

Problem behaviors commonly seen in toddlers and preschoolers include:

❑ Crying, irritability, and temper problems.

❑ Consistent evidence of anxieties and fears.

❑ Toilet problems.

❑ Eating problems.

❑ Bedtime and sleeping problems.

❑ Sexual curiosity problems.

❑ Clinging and other signs of insecurity.

❑ Endless chatter, excessive running around, and other instances of hyperactivity.

❑ Hitting and other acts of aggression.

❑ Disrespect and rudeness.

❑ Unwillingness to share.

❑ A high incidence of trouble with siblings.

❑ Begging, whining, and being demanding and/or bossy.

Different children often show different intensities of each of these behaviors, and most experiment with almost all of them at least once in their first six years. These behaviors usually begin as an aspect of your child's normal development, but they can become severe as a result of environmental stressors, social pressures, or biological problems.

Why Do Kids Have These Problem Behaviors?

To understand why kids act in ways that are often difficult for their parents, it's helpful to look at life from the perspective of your child. Tots and preschoolers believe that they should rule the world and have every right to be self-centered, demanding, and annoying if it suits them. Preschoolers do not believe that there are any consequences to their demands. They often test the limits of their parents' authority by misbehaving, not because they necessarily set out to defy them, but because they believe they have a right to do this and in some ways are *supposed* to do it.

Young toddlers have a developmental need to say "NO," and this can be tough on parents. Much of your child's original self-discovery has been exciting for you to watch (*"I want to watch this. I want to go here. I want to wear this. I want to eat this. I want you mommy."*). What a pleasure it is for a parent to watch their sweet little baby exert his wishes while expressing a pure joy in living! The problem is (and parents often forget this part), that the natural flip side of wanting something is *not* wanting something (*"I don't want this. I don't want to go there. I won't wear it. I won't eat that. GO AWAY!"*). Being capable of saying "NO" is really about saying "I am."

When your child first says "NO" to you, you should sit down and congratulate yourself that your child is developing into an independent human being. After all, aren't we raising our kids so that they can become autonomous, mature adults who are capable of making their own decisions? Remember, no one can succeed in school, refuse drugs, or make meaningful choices in friends or a marriage partner unless she is capable of saying NO.

This first exertion of control can make a toddler drunk with the power of it all. Imagine the feeling of evolving from having had all the decisions made for you to being able to turn your household on its ear and Mommy and Daddy red with one little word. From your toddler's perspective, it almost seems like saying "NO" is all it takes to be king or queen of the world.

This is where the correct parental reaction makes all the difference. If you engage your toddler in a battle of wills, your toddler will decide that his identity is dependent on winning this battle. Parents who react to each "NO" with an insistence that they make every decision for their child are often the same parents who cannot believe how many problem behaviors their child has. If on the other hand, a parent reacts to "NO" with choices (either decision of which would be fine with the parent), nonchalance ("Whatever"), or even a little humor ("No matter what you say I will never allow you to wear that pretty dress to Grandma's"), then their toddler is left with the understanding that it'll take more than one word to master the world.

For some children, their normal problem behaviors resolve relatively quickly as they mature to their next stage of development. For other children, however, what begins as a normal problem behavior erupts into something more serious. Whether this happens depends on a variety of factors, including the child's inborn biological tendencies, her mental and physical health, and the social environment in which she is growing up.

It's the parent's reaction to predictable developmental misbehavior that most often defines whether these behaviors continue, increase, or decrease. The way a parent reacts to a child determines to a high degree how the child turns out. Parents who react to their child with a great deal of anger or with inconsistent or unwise responses run a high risk of creating terribly unhappy kids—and a terribly unhappy home for everyone.

If this is where you stand right now, and if you feel as if you have tried everything you can think of to solve your child's behavioral problems, then you may need a whole new approach to addressing these issues. For example, if you have been screaming or lecturing your child for a while now, it is probably time to admit that this isn't working. Finding a solution to your parenting frustrations will more likely happen if you step back a little. Without a conscious attempt to parent differently, we tend to parent the way we were parented ourselves, including nurturing the way we were nurtured and disciplining the way we were disciplined. Indeed, perhaps the greatest cause of parental mistakes in handling kids stems from an oftentimes unconscious conflict within your own heart and mind over how you were parented.

Being a good parent requires a great deal of time, planning, and energy, but you will not need to become an expert in child development. What you will need is a set of principles that you can apply to the difficult behaviors that most children display as they grow up.

My Three Parenting Principles

The Three Parenting Principles described in the following chapters are literally essential if you want to raise happy, well-adjusted kids. Think of these Three Parenting Principles as the three legs of a stool. If you use only two of the legs, you will fall over. If you don't use any of the legs, you will not be supported and will find yourself on the floor. The Three Principles have evolved from my decades of clinical work, as well as extensive review of hundreds of books and articles about kids and parenting. And they do work. Will these Principles make it so that your child will always behave? Of course not. But you can rest assured that the consistent application of these Principles will help you be the best parent you can be and help your child become the best kid your child can be.

- ❏ **PRINCIPLE #1: BE A SAFE HARBOR**—Create a secure base for your child and ensure that you and your child have a healthy attachment.

- ❏ **PRINCIPLE #2: BE A GOOD BOSS**—Set firm limits and demand in a loving way that your child accept your rules and his or her responsibilities.

- ❏ **PRINCIPLE #3: PREPARE THEM FOR THE REAL WORLD**—Give your child what he needs rather than what he wants and teach him the importance of being part of a larger community.

The urgency in learning and applying the Three Parenting Principles depends upon your circumstances. For example, if you and your family are essentially stress free, if you have no mental or physical conditions that run in your family, if you and your child are completely healthy and happy, and if your family has never experienced any traumas or life tragedies, then your child is much less likely to progress from normal developmental problems to severe behavioral problems. However, even if you are this fortunate, you can still enhance your chances of raising a happy child if you follow the Three Principles. On the other hand, if your home or family has experienced a high degree of stress or adversity or if your child has significant temperamental, biological, or genetic problems, then you run a significant risk of having a child who displays severe problem behaviors. For you, the Three Parenting Principles are a must.

Once you learn about the Three Parenting Principles you may discover that you need to modify or even radically alter your parenting style. This requires changing habits, and habits by definition are hard to break. But using the Three Parenting Principles will give you a peace you may have never experienced before. And, as you adopt these parenting techniques, you will see your child change in wonderful ways. Because each person in your family is an individual and the combination of personalities in your family is unique, you will find that solving problems takes flexibility and imagination. But my Three Parenting Principles are basic to human development, and I will show you how to adapt them to a variety of family characteristics, culture, religion, and beliefs.

I am not suggesting that the Three Principles are going to lead to a utopian existence for you and your family where conflict never arises. Building your family into a cohesive, functioning unit takes work and, at times, involves the honest display of intense emotions. In other words, even the happiest families are going to have their share of thorny moments. But you can rest assured that if you master and adhere to the Three Principles, life with your toddler or preschooler will go much more smoothly and your child will be as well equipped as possible to deal with whatever life sets in her way. Could there be anything more rewarding than that?

The tools and techniques you need are described in the pages that follow. The thing to remember as you move forward is that problem behaviors are very much a natural part of growing up for your child. The key to surviving them and helping your child emerge from them stronger is remembering that these tools are at your disposal. And as you master the use of these tools, you will go a long way toward making life better for everyone in your family.

CHAPTER 2

Parenting Principle #1: Be a Safe Harbor

This principle comes first because it is the foundation on which all healthy parenting is built. Childhood is an incredibly exciting time, but it is also a rocky time marked by intimidating glimpses into the big, bad world and regular encounters with fear of the unknown. Like a ship bucking through storm-tossed seas, your child needs a friendly port where he can return, drop anchor, and be safe until he is ready to set sail again.

When you create a "safe harbor" for your child, you are giving her a sense of security, an understanding that there is someone in the world she can trust and on whom she can rely both physically and emotionally. This safe harbor is a priceless gift that will last her entire life. And if you create that safe harbor for her, you will much more effectively help her to navigate the stormy seas of problem behaviors.

As a safe harbor you must be prepared to provide a special type of encounter with your child. The encounter must include a special intense type of attention that is direct and involves acknowledging your child's unique qualities. Young children are highly sensitive to the type and quality of attention they receive from their parents. Your verbal messages as well as your nonverbal body movements must convey a deep caring and total genuine interest in what he is feeling. During these encounters, you have to let go of all distractions and concentrate on the here-and-now with your child. Be totally present for your child, even if only for a few moments during each encounter. To provide a feeling of safety you must be totally absorbed in a sensitive engagement with your child.

Attachment

At the core of the process of forming a safe harbor is a concept known as attachment. The term "attachment" refers to two interconnected and interdependent concepts: (1) a set of behaviors present in all humans from their first moments of life that is activated when a child feels distressed or in danger to help ensure safety and survival; and (2) the type of closeness and connection a child has with his primary caregiver that depends significantly on the caregiver's response.

Attachment behaviors (crying, clinging, searching, calling, crawling, etc.) allow the child to monitor the whereabouts of and obtain a close proximity to his primary caregiver. These are most highly activated when a child is not physically close to the primary caregiver at a time when he feels distressed or in danger. How the caregiver responds to a child's attachment behaviors will determine whether a child develops a secure or insecure attachment with his caregiver. The type of attachment the child develops will dramatically affect his self-esteem, morals, mental capacity, personality characteristics, emotions, behaviors, relationships with others, and actual brain chemistry. A child who has a good attachment learns to trust his family and the world enough to grow up healthy and happy. A child who has a bad attachment does not trust others and learns to manipulate, cover up, fight, and control the world to survive emotionally.

A healthy attachment allows a child to develop good social skills, good emotional health, good thinking skills, and good morals. When attached in a healthy way to her primary caregiver, a child develops a way to self-soothe, a good feeling about herself, trust and respect for others, and a belief that she has an important role within her family and the world.

There are two essential ingredients necessary for an adult and child to become attached in a healthy way: the adult must be dependably available and present over time, and the adult must be responsive, sensitive, and emotionally invested in interactions with the child.

A child can have a primary attachment with a person other than his biological mother and/or father. He can have a primary attachment with an adoptive parent, a grandparent, an aunt or uncle, a foster parent or any other adult who is consistently dependable, stable, and invested in his care.

The Four Phases of Attachment

Although the process of attachment between a child and his parents is lifelong, the first three-to-five years of his life are most important because of the degree of dependency he has on his parents and their ability during this time to influence the child's view of how he sees himself. During this time, attachment evolves in four relatively predictable phases.

PHASE ONE

The first phase happens around birth and lasts until approximately two-to-three months. During this phase, a baby learns to respond to humans in general. He is beginning to orient himself and to learn how to figure out through his senses of sight and smell what a human face and voice are and how to respond to them. Within this first phase, the infant does not show any particularly strong preference for a single attachment figure.

PHASE TWO

The second phase begins gradually at the age of two-to-three months and lasts until the child is approximately seven months old. During this phase, a process of complex behavior begins to be directed toward one or more figures (including crying when the caregiver leaves and stopping crying when the caregiver returns).

PHASE THREE

The third phase begins between six and nine months and lasts until the child is approximately three years old. During this phase, the young child strives to maintain closeness with one or more caregivers through locomotion, direct communication, and other direct social signals. Three primary attachment behaviors are used:

❑ Maintaining proximity (staying near and resisting separations from the attachment figure).

❑ Finding a safe harbor (turning to the attachment figure for comfort and support).

❑ Establishing a secure base (using the attachment figure as a base from which to engage in play and explore his world).

PHASE FOUR

The fourth phase begins between two-and-a-half and three years of age. Through language and interaction, the child begins to see the world from the perspective of both himself and his attachment figure. During the fourth phase the child incorporates the goals, plans, and desires of his attachment figure into his own decision making, which results in shared plans and activities. Toward the third birthday, a child is increasingly able to recognize, understand, and talk about the feelings and behaviors of family members. By three, most children understand increasingly complex rules for social interaction, are able to interpret others' feelings and goals, and use such rules to affect others' emotions.

What Is an Example of a Good Attachment?

Mary is a newborn. She is cold, tired, hungry, and afraid of the lights and noise. She cries. Her mother promptly picks her up and comforts her. Mary's mom looks lovingly in her eyes, gently touches and strokes her, smiles and coos to her, rocks her, and feeds her. A host of chemicals in Mary's brain release and flood her with a sense of pleasure, relaxation, and well-being. Over the next twelve months this pattern is repeated hundreds and hundreds of times. Gradually Mary becomes convinced, "Wow, I cry and my mommy comes and helps me. . . . I can depend on my mommy to help and protect me." Mary has learned to *trust* her mother.

Mary is now about a year old and for the next couple of years she has lots of self-centered wants. She wants constant attention and toys and things. She wants to touch and do everything at the exact moment she thinks about wanting it. Her mother decides which of these are good for her and which are not. She gently guides her away from some of these and firmly says "no" to those that are dangerous or not good for her. Mary senses the following, "Wow, my mommy doesn't let me have every single thing I want. When I get really mad at her because she doesn't give me what I want, she doesn't give in to me. But she always stays with me, even when I have a fit. I can trust my mommy to be here for me and to know what is best for me. I feel safe knowing she is looking out for me."

Mary is securely attached to her mother. During the first three years of Mary's life, she and her mother have had countless interactions involving direct eye contact, skin-to-skin touching, rocking and reassuring stroking, comfort and nurturance, and soothing vocalizing. Mary's mom is sensitive to Mary's rhythms, cues, and states of mind, including smiles, glances, gestures, and the meaning behind her various cries.

Mary has learned important life lessons over her first three years through her attachment with her mother. She has learned to trust someone and she has learned that she can depend on her mommy. Mary has also learned to self-soothe through this attachment. When Mary's mommy uses a warm facial expression, a relaxed posture and a soft tone of voice, Mary receives stimulation that allows her brain to grow in a way that helps her with her own self-regulation. When Mary's immature unorganized nervous system becomes aroused when she is upset and crying, her mom provides an understandable, consistent message to soothe her. Over time, the repetition of this allows Mary to become biologically able to regulate her own upset emotions.

How Does a Healthy Attachment Compare to an Unhealthy Attachment?

Imagine that two little baby boys are born on the same day at two different areas of a frozen lake. On one end of the lake Jim drops from the sky onto the cold snowy ice and begins to shiver with fright. Almost immediately a soft and cuddly man scoops him up and wraps him in a warm fuzzy blanket. He carries him across the frozen pond to a nearby warm cabin. Soon he is being rocked and sung to and fed warm milk, all the while being looked upon by gentle loving eyes. The man tenderly tells him he is to be called "Daddy." When Jim cries from pain or hunger or loneliness, Daddy seems to know what to do. As Jim grows a little older he finds that sometimes his Daddy says "no" to him, but he learns to accept the limits because he knows his Daddy means well and Jim has learned to trust him. Over the next few years Jim begins to believe that he must be a wonderful person because, he reasons, "If Daddy is always here for me then I must be worth loving."

On the other end of the lake Ted also drops from the sky and begins to shiver with fright. A woman comes to pick him up but she's preoccupied so she seems kind of stiff and distant. She carries Ted to a different cabin, but doesn't take much time to hold or rock him. Sometimes when he shivers and cries she doesn't seem to notice. At other times she almost scares him with how much she hovers over him. Ted learns that his cries may or may not bring comfort. Sometimes Ted is scolded and ridiculed for wanting to be held or comforted. This makes him really angry and sad. As Ted grows a little older he is sometimes allowed to wander a long way into the woods unnoticed. Strangers sometimes watch him when he is far from home. Ted learns how to charm these strangers so that they will give him what he wants. Ted never really knows what to expect from mommy—sometimes when she comes to get him she loads him with praise and toys. At other times, when he clings desperately to her, she seems to be furious at him. Sometimes when he screams that he wants something she gives it to him. Other times she ignores him or yells at him or hits him. Ted learns that if he wants his needs met he must do it himself because, he reasons, he is about the only one he can truly trust. As Ted grows up, he thinks deep down that he is a bad person because, "If Mommy doesn't care much about me I must not be worth much."

Ted was attached to his mother, but not in a healthy way. Human infants form attachments to a caregiver as long as there is a consistent person to interact with, even if they are mistreated. Kids are unattached only when there is absolutely no stable person to interact with on a regular basis. This is rare and happens only in environments like orphanages or among children who are repeatedly switched to different foster care sites.

A child who has not received the components of a healthy attachment is used to being hurt, disappointed, or afraid—so he projects these feelings onto new relationships and becomes angry or aggressive toward others. Children who are always rejected, who receive inconsistent comfort, or who are cared for by frightening caregivers are the most likely to show intensely demanding, aggressive, and angry responses. Their anger usually continues as they grow into older children and adults.

Infants raised by sensitive, available caregivers learn they can readily get their needs met and that they have an effect on the world. Children who receive unpredictably unresponsive, unavailable, or insensitive care often become overly dependent on others and have trouble regulating their moods. They often feel intensely anxious, angry, and sad. Insecurely attached preschoolers are more socially withdrawn, less likely to show sympathy for injured or unhappy playmates, are less willing to interact with friendly adults, and are more likely to display aggression and disobedience.

How Can I Help My Child Feel More Attached?

Here are some general ways to help ensure you and other close family members develop a secure attachment with your child. If you follow these, you will go a long way toward mastering Principle #1.

❏ **EMOTIONAL AVAILABILITY FROM YOU EARLY** in your child's life is essential. Early attachment relationships influence a child's developing personality.

❏ **SPEND AS MUCH TIME AS POSSIBLE** physically close to your child. If your child begins to act up in any way, first think, "I wonder if I have spent enough quality time with my youngster today." Throughout the toddler and preschool years, your child needs as much of your presence as you can possibly give.

❏ **HOW YOU THINK OF YOUR** child when she is distressed often makes a difference in how you respond to your child. A mother who sees her fussy child as acting this way to bother her is likely to respond with impatience or rejection, while another who attributes the fussiness to temporary distress that the parent can help alleviate is more likely to respond with comfort.

❏ **IMPROVING YOUR LIFE CIRCUMSTANCES OR** seeking effective support from others may allow you to respond more sensitively to your child's attachment needs. This is a critical time in your child's life. If your personal situation is preventing you from offering the kind of attachment he needs, do what you can to change your personal situation.

❏ **DOING EVERYTHING IN YOUR POWER** to lower the stress level in your family has enormous implications for your young child. Families filled with high stress tend to be associated with more insensitive, harsh, rejecting, inconsistent, or unpredictable parenting behaviors. This kind of parenting fosters the development of a child's insecure attachment and can cause serious problems in a child's behavior and personality development.

❏ **IT IS SOMETIMES DIFFICULT FOR** both parents to be actively involved with a child. Very young children can do very well as long as they have a healthy attachment to at least one parent— the one spending a great deal of time with the child.

❏ **GRANDPARENTS, OR OTHER FAMILY MEMBERS** can also play an important role. For example, they can help provide a child with feelings of security. If a young child is repeatedly picked up by a grandparent while distressed, is held on his lap, is soothed while leaning against his chest, is talked to with comforting words, the child will think, "when I feel sad grandpa comforts me. I am important to grandpa so I must be a valued person." The child then carries these thoughts over to what he expects in relationships with others, such as teachers and close friends and develops the belief that the world is a trustworthy, meaningful, predictable and controllable place.

Being a safe harbor for your child takes work and diligence and—above everything else—time. There is no substitute for being there for your child. And there is no more powerful or satisfying message that you can send to your child than, "I am here for you."

And if you have a healthy attachment with your child, you will find that there is little in the world that can measure up to this. One of the true joys of parenting is realizing that you have become someone that your child can rely on and that you are the person he looks to for guidance and security.

The next chapter looks at specific problem behaviors and shows you how the effective use of Principle #1 can help you to deal with them.

CHAPTER 3

Putting Principle #1 to Work

Securely attached children have a positive self-image and tend to grow up to be compassionate, empathetic, affectionate, resilient, capable of intimacy, and able to self-regulate their emotions in a healthy way. The following problem behaviors tend to be those that are most affected or worsened if a child lacks a strong sense of safety, feels insecure, or feels a sense of high stress or distress in his life. They can be lessened if one or both parents strive to obtain a more secure attachment with their children. While attending to the two Principles you will learn later in this book may also lessen the intensity of the following problem behaviors, initially pay the most attention to Principle #1, as enhancing your attachment with your child is likely the most effective course to take.

The following problem behaviors commonly seen in toddlers and preschoolers will be covered in this chapter:

❏ Bedtime resistance

❏ Breath holding

❏ Clinging

❏ Day care stresses

❏ Early awakening

❏ Excessive crying

❏ Fears and anxieties

❏ Hyperactivity

❏ Irritability and crankiness

❏ Meltdowns

❏ Nailbiting, thumb sucking, and extensive use of a pacifier

❏ Nightmares and night terrors

❏ Night waking

❏ Regression—"acting like a baby"

❏ Sleepwalking

Bedtime Resistance

Getting your child to settle down and go to sleep is a very common problem in young children. Almost 20 percent of kids aged one through three and approximately 10 percent of children aged four and five have these sleep problems. These problems—and the lack of sleep that comes with them—are often linked to several other problem behaviors, and they affect how the family functions and frequently negatively affect a parent's health.

The first step in handling bedtime resistance is to provide your child with a bedtime routine. Nighttime routines are critical to helping your child feel like you are a safe harbor. These should last about 30 to 40 minutes and can include taking a bath, brushing teeth, reading stories, talking in a darkened bedroom, saying prayers, singing gentle songs, and so on. You should also choose whether the bedtime routine includes an open or closed door when you leave, whether the lights are on or off during this time, and other things of this sort. You must be consistent whenever possible—sticking to the prescribed routine creates a safe feeling in your child. You must decide all these factors ahead of time and then tell your child what the rules are. Explain that if he does not stick with the rules, you will cut short the routine for that night (leaving before the time you agreed you would stay in the room, reading fewer books, etc.). A security object (also referred to as a snuggley, lovey, comfort toy, etc.) makes a wonderful transition object that can bring enormous comfort to your young child. A security object is a healthy tool for your child and should be encouraged and *never* ridiculed. He can use this security object when he is or feels alone, when he needs to find his own comfort, or when he needs a special companion. Your child's security object can be an indispensable part of the bedtime routine. For example, you can say to your toddler, "Go and get your special friend and hug him while we read. Then when I leave the room, you can hug him instead of me until I return in the morning."

If you decide that your child's bedtime routine includes your staying with him until he is asleep, be sure to lie down on or beside his bed fully clothed and on top of the covers. This will allow him to understand that you are merely staying until your agreed on departure time and that you do not plan to stay all night. Do not promise or imply otherwise. If you do, he might feel that you have abandoned him if he wakes and you are not there.

You must make it clear to your child that after you have finished your bedtime routine you view it as unacceptable if your child leaves his bedroom, turns on the light to play, or wanders around the house. Of course the parent can explain to the child that in the case of an emergency or sudden onset of illness, these rules do not apply. However, it is best to incorporate requests like "I want a drink of water" or "I have to go to the bathroom" into the nighttime routine. This will avoid the child's ability to manipulate or control the situation after the parent has said goodnight. Describe to your child what a good sleeper is, and that you know that he can sleep through the night.

If your toddler deliberately wants to stay awake in his bed after you have completed your bedtime routine, then that is his choice and you need to honor it. You can successfully tell a child to get into bed and stay there, but you can never command him to fall asleep. He may want to make a point to you that he is in charge of his body by humming, singing, sitting up, whistling, or otherwise insisting that he will not go to sleep. If he does this, just close the door so that his transgressions do not unnecessarily disturb the rest of the family. He will fall asleep soon enough, probably earlier if he is convinced that you are not bothered by his noises. To help him along, you may want to use a reward system, perhaps stickers for each night he does well that can be "cashed in" at a predetermined point for a special treat.

Breath Holding

Infants, toddlers, and young children learn what helps them control their environment through a method of trial and error. Those behaviors they find that work in controlling their powerful parents are kept. Those behaviors that do not are abandoned. Sometimes a child stumbles onto breath holding as a way to obtain an incredible amount of attention from her parents. The reaction of her parents will determine the degree to which she will continue using this technique. If during and after this attempt for full attention, her parents seem nonchalant or uninterested, then very quickly she will set out to find another behavior that works more successfully. The best way to employ Principle #1 here is to try to distract your child by offering her a glass of juice or an extra hug if you sense that an upsetting event may be leading her to holding her breath.

Remember the following as a way to allow you to maintain an excellent poker face during your child's experimentation with breath holding: it is impossible to commit suicide by holding one's breath. If your child continues the breath holding episode to the point of a light sleep, normal breathing will take over and she will recover in full health without any negative physical impact. When the event is over give your child a brief hug and try to act as if nothing significant has happened.

Clinging

Toddlers and preschoolers use you as a secure base from which they can explore their world. At a point of separation, if a child does not feel he can trust that his attachment figure will return as promised, he might resort to clinging in an effort to prevent the separation he fears. A toddler clings for two main reasons: (1) he temporarily lacks confidence in his ability to face the world without being by your side or (2) he believes doing so will snag him more consistent or better quality care from you. If your toddler is clinging to you, it is critically important that you not refuse or reject this if at all possible. Your behaviors toward your child should be filled with actions that promote attachment (gentle facial expressions, direct eye contact, a reassuring calm voice, gentle touch, hugs and stroking, etc.).

The parent who gradually lengthens the time between leaving and returning (beginning with a few seconds and increasing gradually to minutes, then hours) teaches the growing child to increase his patience for the relieving event of seeing his parent once again.

Routines (for example, always hugging or kissing the same way or saying the same phrase before leaving) will help your child tremendously to trust that you will always come back.

Development can be inhibited or prevented but it cannot be forced. You cannot force your child into being more independent before he is ready. In fact, pushing your child to be more separate usually has the opposite effect of making him cling even more. Studies have shown that the more irritable, scolding, and impatient a mother is with her overly dependent child, the more clinging the child tends to be. Only when a child feels that he can totally depend on his safe harbor will he feel comfortable enough to venture away and strike out on his own without his parent close to him.

Realistically you cannot always be there for your growing child. This is where a security object can prove invaluable. Since he is using the object as a temporary replacement for the security he has experienced with you, his attachment to this object is really a compliment to you for having shown him the importance of feeling secure. You should help him take care of it and protect him from society's inevitable ridicule when they see him carry it in public. If his security object gets dirty or ragged, work with him on how to wash it, fix it or sew it back to some semblance of acceptability. If he wants to carry around a blanket that is too large, help him to trim it to a more acceptable size. You are acting like a safe harbor when you respect his love affair with and need for his cherished transitional object. Rest assured that by age six or seven most children have learned to replace the comfort they have obtained from their security object with different toys or with relationships with other children.

Day Care Stresses

A recent government study found that by the age of three, more than two-thirds of toddlers and preschoolers have spent a substantial amount of time in the care of someone other than their parents. Many children begin their experience in day care at the age of three months. The average number of hours of day care for toddlers and preschoolers is about 33 hours a week.

Government researchers have found (after correcting for various factors known to affect the parent-child bond) that the more time an infant spends in day care the less sensitive the parent and the less engaged the child seemed to be. But the differences were small and seemed to disappear as the child grew to age four. The researchers also found that those who spent more than 30 hours per week in day care were more likely to be highly aggressive (demanding attention, disobeying, arguing, crying, hitting other children).

So should parents feel guilty or alter their plan for working outside the home? No. But what parents should do is try if at all possible is to parent in ways that will overcome any potential problems that day care generates.

One of the most effective ways to offset parental guilt and remove any negative effect on your child from spending a lot of time in day care is to use Principle #1 and absolutely promise yourself that you will spend a minimum of 15 to 20 minutes of undivided time each and every day with each of your children. This is absolutely critical to promoting trust, good mental health, and a good parent-child relationship. If this seems like an impossible goal, you need to reprioritize your life so that you can make this happen. What are you doing now that you can eliminate so that you can find this time? How much value can you place on your ability to look yourself in the mirror each night and know that you are being a good parent?

Evaluate the day care facility you are using carefully. It is important—especially if your child is going to be spending a great deal of time in day care—to try to find a facility with a low staff turnover rate. He will be forming an attachment relationship with the care provider and if this person is regularly changing, it could have a harmful effect on him. When your child starts attending a new facility, try to schedule the first few days to stay with him. If the site does not allow this, ask yourself why. Staying for a couple of days at the beginning, and then gradually decreasing the amount of time you stay with him will bring both of you peace of mind: you because you will be able to assure yourself that this place is good, and your child will be able to associate you more with the site and be able to warm up slowly to the staff while he has you still there as his safe harbor from which he can explore.

Early Awakening

Most children age two to three need a minimum of 12 to 13 hours of sleep a night. Preschoolers need a minimum of 10 to 12 hours of sleep a night. Toddlers and preschoolers who sleep less than 10 to 11 hours in a 24-hour period frequently have more opposi-tional, hyperactive and aggressive behaviors. Therefore making sure your child sleeps enough is critical.

Some toddlers and preschoolers awaken between 5:00 and 6:00 and are fully awake and ready to go before their parents are ready to arise. They call from their crib, bed, or bedroom and are ready to rev up for the day—they are your typical "morning people." Most of these children have received plenty of sleep and are no longer tired. If this applies to your child and he is sleeping more than his required number of hours, you may want to evaluate how to decrease the amount of sleep your child obtains during the day (naps) or change the time you are putting him to bed. If this does-n't work, explain to your child that unless there is a true emer-gency, that there is a firm rule that he cannot leave his bedroom until you come to get him. Children four and older are easily able to play quietly until allowed to leave their room. Place a clock in his room and show him what the time must be before he can come out. Tell your two-to-three-year-old that he is to read or play quietly in his room until you come to get him. Give him specific books, toys, or activities to do until then. If you are changing a pattern of previously allowing your child to come to your bed very early in the morning, set a clock radio to play music to indicate when you will allow him to come in. You may want to add a praise system of a "star" for each morning he does well, and reward him with a small treat or special food when he achieves a certain number of "stars."

Being a safe harbor and having a secure attachment includes providing a predictable routine. If your child understands your rules of early awakening, the predictability of these rules helps him feel a sense of security and safety. Remember that a child must have his basic needs met before he can develop a sense of security. This also applies to the parent. If a child's getting up too early and awakening the parent are directly contributing to the parent's lack of adequate rest, it is essential to the attachment relationship for the parent to fix this since stressed-out, inadequately rested parents do not make good attachment figures.

Excessive Crying

All children experience stress of one type or another no matter how excellent their parents are at parenting or how hard their parents try to prevent stress in their environment. Crying serves a good purpose in that it allows a child to release harmful stress hormones. Parents sometimes try to prevent their child from crying because crying may make the parent feel uncomfortable. However, you should not do this. Crying (and being able to express one's emotions) allows a child to feel better, act better, heal physically faster, and avoid stress related illnesses.

Children should be allowed to cry. Following crying and the release of harmful stress hormones, the body is able to achieve a highly relaxed state. Crying helps to get rid of the excess hormones that can make a child chronically anxious, overactive, and angry. Emotional crying produces tears that are actually filled with stress hormones which, if allowed to build up, can increase your child's chances of depression and damage her body's ability to heal and recover.

If at all possible within the parent's comfort level, children should be held gently or be in close physical proximity to the parent while they cry. Isolation or withdrawal of attention during their cry can be perceived by the child as abandonment and/or punishment. They may perceive that their parent is withdrawing their love and attention just when they need it the most—this can result in a very painful emotion and may increase their need for more crying.

Fears and Anxieties

Fears in your child cannot be avoided. Nor should they be. Fears help prevent your children from being exposed to dangers they are not yet ready to handle. It is healthy for toddlers to be afraid of strangers, dogs, noisy environments, and separation from their primary care providers. They should not be told to kiss every stranger, pet every dog, or be scolded when they cry with a stranger's approach.

Some fears and anxieties are predictable based upon the age of your child. For example if your child is:

❏ Eight-to-eighteen months, she is commonly afraid of separation, strangers, loud noises, crowds, and water.

❏ Two years old, she is commonly afraid of loud sounds, large objects, going down the drain, and animals.

❏ Two-and-a-half-years old, she is commonly afraid of familiar objects being moved and unexpected events.

❏ Three years old, she is commonly afraid of masks, senior people, the dark, and animals.

❏ Four years old, she is commonly afraid of loud noises, the dark, wild animals, separations, imaginary creatures, threats, and aggressive actions.

❏ Five years old, she is commonly afraid of injuries, her own blood, falls, and dogs.

Parents should acknowledge their child's fears without adding to them. Understand that her fear is real to her, even if it is not realistic from an adult perspective. Do not attempt to argue with your child about her fears, or trivialize or ridicule them. Respect her wish to withdraw and avoid the source of her fears—*never* push her toward facing the thing she fears. Fears drop off faster if they are treated with respect by parents. Reassure and provide a safe harbor. Give her warm hugs and let her know that you will help her take control over the fear and help her avoid the source of her fears.

The following are the most typical categories of fears with added hints on how to avoid and handle them:

ABANDONMENT FEARS

Fear of abandonment is actually the greatest fear of all children— the fear of being unloved or left by parents. When a child experiences or faces a separation from the primary attachment figure, she needs reassurance of a return. In addition, parents should *never* threaten a child with abandonment—never, never, never. Don't even use it in casual ways ("If you don't come now I'll leave you here"), no matter how angry or tired or frustrated you feel.

Regular, predictable presences and absences with accompanying predictable leaving routines are the best ways to prevent your child from realizing her worst fear. If your schedule forces you to deviate from your regular routine, if at all possible you should prepare your child in advance for the change. Kids can handle separations much more easily if they have been fully prepared ahead of time. *Never* leave unexpectedly by sneaking away to avoid their wails of sadness.

STRESSFUL FEARS

Young children are often not able to express how upset they are about tensions in their homes or environments. The healthy toddler or preschooler who suddenly has profuse and varied fears, who increasingly dissolves into tears, who suddenly refuses to leave the house, or who is unable to achieve things he used to do easily may be frightened at the prospect (real or imagined) that the life she knows is ending. Speaking of these fears can be next to impossible for a young child. She will only be able to show you how scared she is through her behaviors.

If you see this in your child, it is essential that you provide her with the greatest possible comfort and feeling of safety. Increase your holding, rocking, eye contact, soothing conversations, and reassurances. Let your child know that even if things around her may seem unstable, you will always provide her with a safe harbor/secure base that she can trust and depend on.

MODELED FEARS

Parents act as role-models for their children. The way they act may determine whether a child becomes fearful when facing a new situation. For example, when a child first meets a stranger, many children will begin to wail with fright and look to their parents for their reaction. If the parents are calm and reassuring, the child will take great solace in his parents' evaluation and relax. If, on the other hand, if the parents look worried, the child will likely erupt in fearful screams.

If you suspect that your child has modeled her fear of something by watching an important person in her life react with an intense emotion, you can help your child tremendously by interacting with her in a reassuring way. Allow her to watch you deal calmly with a similar event or thing. If this is especially difficult for you to do, let her watch another important person interact with this feared substance coolly. For example, if you have an aversion to spiders, but your child has amplified your dislike to an almost disabling point, find a trusted family member or friend who can gently and sensitively model a realistic reaction to bugs.

REALISTIC FEARS

Sometimes in spite of your best efforts to protect your child, life delivers a cruel experience. Your child may have been bitten by a dog, had a close brush with drowning, or watched a neighbor's house burn. The fears and reactions as a result of this experience can be dramatic and disabling and can be amplified or extrapolated to other fears. For example, a child bitten by a dog may deeply fear all animals.

Treatment should include sympathetic and reassuring conversations and the patience of waiting for time to diminish the memories. It may work to very slowly (based upon your child's reactions) introduce the dreaded thing back to her life (a two-inch wading pool for the child who almost drowned or a big stuffed dog for the child who was bitten). But under no circumstances should a child be forced prematurely back to the dreaded experience in a misguided attempt to desensitize your child's fears. This action will only backfire and entrench a lifelong fear in his heart.

Hyperactivity

The problem behavior of hyperactivity in children may be one of three things:

❏ Normal childhood active behaviors.

❏ Normal behaviors for a child who has this specific temperament.

❏ Early signs of Attention Deficit Hyperactivity Disorder (ADHD).

Hyperactivity may be related to the fact that young preschool children are normally active and energetic and tend to flit from one activity to another. Sometimes parents worry that their child is hyperactive when he is merely showing the normal activities of young children.

Hyperactivity may also be related to the temperament of high activity, meaning that the child is biologically born to be more active than other children. Temperament is discussed at length in Appendix 2.

Hyperactivity may also be one of the first emerging signs of ADHD or another mental health condition (see Chapter 8 and Appendix #3 for more details). One of the requirements for an eventual diagnosis of ADHD in a school age child is that he showed signs and symptoms before the age of seven. Children who will be diagnosed with ADHD may show beginning signs as early as age three or four or even earlier. These signs include a high level and intensity of many of the following symptoms: distractibility, difficulties with concentration, inattention, acting before thinking, acting "on the go" all the time, and showing an excessive amount of fidgeting or squirming. One of the reasons, though, that few clinicians make a formal diagnosis of ADHD in preschoolers is that it is difficult to determine whether these symptoms are age related, temperament related or disorder related.

What is a normal length of time you can expect toddlers or preschoolers to stay put on one activity before changing to the next? A normal attention span is about three-to-five minutes per year of your child's age. This means that a two-year-old should be able to focus on an activity between six and ten minutes before moving on to the next activity. A four-year-old should be able to remain focused on one activity for between 12 and 20 minutes. Note that attention span does *not* apply to the activity of watching a television program or playing video games. A child is really not ready to tackle the demands of first grade until he can remain captivated or focused on one non-electronic activity for a minimum of at least 20 minutes.

Your main approaches to dealing with "wilding" based upon Principle #1 include:

❑ **ACCEPTING YOUR CHILD'S OVERLY ACTIVE** behaviors as part of who he is. Don't allow yourself or others to label him as "bad" because of his increased energy or overly active behaviors. Remember that his high activity and short attention span are likely due to his biology. Your child did not select his temperament as a way to bug you. He desperately needs you to be a sensitive and responsive safe harbor.

❑ **PROVIDE AN OUTLET FOR HIS RELEASE** of energy. He has the energy inside him and desperately needs a way to release it. An important role for you as the parent is to actually schedule into his daily routine a way to use up this extra energy. This means *every* day. If you don't do this, his extra energy will spill out in negative behaviors. Of course, the more you do with him the more tightly you will bond with your child, since highly active kids deeply appreciate a parent who does activities with them.

❑ **KEEP YOUR HOME WELL ORGANIZED.** Regular predictable routines are extremely important to highly active kids. When they know what is coming (when the nap and bedtime is, when their meals are, when their daily activity is) they are more able to adjust their energy bursts to the appropriate times.

❑ **AVOID FATIGUE AND HUNGER IN** your child. When hyperactive toddlers and preschoolers become hungry or exhausted they tend to lash out in highly active or aggressive ways. Many experts believe that hyperactivity is significantly worsened by sleep deprivation. Do not wait to put your child to bed when he seems or acts tired. Assume your child needs more sleep than other children his age and schedule sleep for him as if his health depends on it.

❑ **TRY TO STRETCH YOUR CHILD'S** attention span. Set aside brief periods every day where you can read to him to help him regulate the need to learn to sit still and listen. Play quiet games to help him learn the social skills of quieting his twitching muscles. Praise him for his calmness, even if relatively brief. If he gets restless again stop and begin again at a later time—preferably at a regularly scheduled time he can expect and can internally prepare for.

Irritability and Crankiness

A fussy or irritable toddler or preschooler can place a severe stress on your emotional well-being, especially if you place great pride in your parenting skills. First, have your child evaluated for physical causes of any chronic or constant irritability. Remember that childhood depression can present in toddlers and preschoolers this way. Ask your healthcare provider to make sure he doesn't have signs of depression, side effects to medications he is taking, chronic disease (allergies, ear infections, gastrointestinal problems), or developmental delays. Sometimes irritable or cranky kids serve as beacons of high family stress.

Chronically cranky or irritable toddlers and preschoolers can set up a negative attachment cycle with their parents. This cycle looks like this: the child displays difficult behaviors that are difficult to be around . . . the parent reacts with a strong negative emotion that creates an intense but unsatisfying connection . . . subsequently both child and parent distance themselves from each other and their connection suffers.

Instead the parent needs to override his own natural tendency to avoid his child's difficult behavior and force himself to promote attachment-enhancing behaviors, especially those involving touch. When parents do this, the negative attachment cycle can be stopped. Touch is a form of security to a child. Touching your child is one of the best ways to calm a cranky toddler or preschooler. Think of his irritability or crankiness as a request for more touch. Do this even if it doesn't come naturally to you. Sometimes just changing your mindset works miracles.

Meltdowns

Sometimes your toddler or preschooler seems to dissolve into a form of insanity, a seemingly uncontrollable sobbing and terrifying loss of civilized behavior. During such times, no matter what a parent may say to try and stop it, absolutely nothing works. These meltdowns frequently occur at extremely inopportune moments (waiting in a line at the supermarket or airport, when you are at a holiday family gathering, etc.). This difficult behavior often occurs as a result of your child's profound sensory overload and exhaustion. Basically, your child has reached an overtiredness that is close to madness. He is so deeply fatigued that his ability to make sense of his world is totally destroyed. All he can do is cry as deeply as would a distressed infant. When the adults in his life perceive him as being ornery and seek to punish him, he becomes even more filled with terror. Your child hates displeasing his parents, but he has no clue how to stop it and threats only make him feel worse and more out of control.

The only way to successfully handle a child in the midst of a meltdown is to get in touch with your own inevitable feelings of rage when you see him "lose it." Your child needs his safe harbor now more than ever. He needs to feel a strong gentle embrace around him (in spite of his raging, writhing, squirming panic). He needs to hear something like the following: "Yes, honey, I know you are totally exhausted. It's scary to feel tired and mixed up about everything. I'll hold you until you are able to settle down and relax."

Nail Biting, Thumb Sucking, and Extensive Use of a Pacifier

All babies suck their thumb or fingers. The habit is routine for infants and toddlers. Many preschoolers suck their thumbs or fingers (though by the age of four only one in six preschoolers does). There are few if any reasons to be concerned about this. Most dentists reassure their parents that there is no negative effect of thumb or finger sucking on your child's dental health until permanent teeth come in at age six or seven. Think of thumb or finger sucking as an excellent way your child has discovered to relieve his own stress—a way for him to help him cope with his tensions. Whether or not this normal habit continues into toddler and preschool years is dependent to a large degree on the reaction of a child's parents. If parents zero in on and focus inordinate attention to the habit, it will become a huge problem.

Yanking the fingers out of your child's mouth whenever you pass, forcing a child to wear mittens, or placing a bitter solution on his fingers against his will do not work and will only frighten a child or make him think that he has more power in the relationship than his parent. Seeking to bribe your child to stop sucking his fingers or thumb is often useless, unless the child can be convinced that he would not be receiving the "spoils" any other way than by quitting this habit.

If your child is six months to one year old, you still have the option of deciding if you want to offer him a pacifier if this seems more socially acceptable to you. The advantages of having your child suck a pacifier is that there are more subtle tricks you can use to help him get rid of the habit at an earlier age than his thumb. For example, you can tie the pacifier to the bed or his security object so that he uses it only when he is with these things. But do not get into a power struggle. Also do not abruptly remove the pacifier without preparation—this can negatively affect his trust of you.

Principle #1 is all about providing an environment for your child so he can feel safe, protected, and stress free. All babies use some kind of self-soothing device when they are not in immediate proximity to their primary caregiver or when, even in the presence of their primary caregiver, they need an additional way to feel safe or express their distress. Sucking is a comforting biological behavior that equates with safety and nurturing. It's a biological need to promote well-being. If a baby or child sucks things, he is really saying he has found a way to help himself self-soothe. Parents should rejoice in this. But they should also view it as a symptom signal that their child is not feeling safe or that he is feeling overstressed. If not viewed this way, the sucking behavior may turn into a way the child attempts to control the emotions of the parent.

Nail biting, seen most commonly in children age three to five, often occurs as a result of life pressures. Try not to worry about the habit itself. Instead, take note of when your child does this. Does he bite his nails only in front of you to bug you? If so, you should read again the text under thumb sucking because the same advice applies here. Does your child bite his nails when he faces high stress or tension? If so, is there something you can do to help him deal with this? Do not focus on the nail biting, but instead focus on fixing the issues that bring him stress.

Nightmares and Night Terrors

Nightmares are scary dreams that may awaken your child at night. When toddlers or preschoolers have a nightmare they frequently cry or scream or run to their parents' bed. Toddlers frequently have nightmares about issues around separation from their parents, and preschoolers frequently have nightmares about monsters or the dark. If your child has an occasional nightmare, hug her, reassure her, and perhaps sit on her bed until she is calm. You can offer her things like nightlights or "magic objects" beside her bed to help. Do not spend a lot of time and energy hunting down the "monster" in her room because this tends to suggest to the child that something was really there. Most children return to sleep quite quickly after receiving reassurance from their safe harbor.

Night terrors are when your child is agitated or restless during her sleep and she cannot be awakened or comforted. Your child may sit up suddenly and scream in terror or talk wildly. Your child is not aware that you are with her, and she cannot remember what happened in the morning. The episode usually happens one or two hours after she goes to sleep and may last approximately 10 to 30 minutes. If you discover a pattern of regular night terrors at a specific time in the evening, you may want to wake your child up 15 minutes before the expected onset of the terror and give her a long hug and stay with her for approximately five minutes (perhaps singing a song or reading a story) before you allow her to fall back to sleep. Night terrors often occur if your child is getting overtired during the day. You may have to restart afternoon naps, institute a one-hour "quiet time" in the afternoon, or institute earlier bedtimes.

Nightmares and night terrors are usually a way for children to deal with difficult emotions they feel unable to express in the daytime. Review your child's life to see if there is anything that may be scaring her and whether you can alter it. Is she playing too wildly with older children? Is she being too harshly or frequently disciplined? Is she watching violent video games or television especially close to bedtime? If she remembers her scary dream during the day, you can discuss it and help her come up with a better ending. If she experiences a recurring nightmare, do not seek to dissect the content of it, but instead take note that there is undoubtedly a major stressor in her life and work hard to diminish that. During this time, your striving to maintain her nighttime routine will make her feel safer.

Night Waking

After the first few months of life, a child's sleeping pattern is a learned social behavior, just as eating three meals a day (as opposed to two or four) is a learned social behavior. If you remember this, you will understand why parents must teach the social appropriateness of learning to sleep for long stretches at night (rather than regularly waking and playing in the middle of the night). Your child must learn that even if he awakens in the middle of the night, it is socially expected for her to fall back asleep unaided until morning.

All toddlers and preschoolers are perfectly capable of learning how to put themselves back to sleep independently if they wake up in the middle of the night. If your young toddler is still in a crib and you hear her cry, briefly check on the child to be sure she is not ill or hurt. You can reassure your child by patting her gently, lovingly, and briefly on the head or back and saying something like, "Honey, we all need to sleep when it is nighttime. I checked on you to make sure you were safe. Now I am leaving, and you must go back to sleep. Hug your 'snuggle' instead of me. It can help you get back to sleep." Do not stay in the room for more than 30 seconds. Typically, a child will scream after this for quite a while—perhaps three or four hours the first night. The second night, it might be two or three hours. The periods will get increasingly shorter after this until she learns that she must go back to sleep herself. While it might be painful to hear your child cry this way, this experience will cause her no harm. In fact, your child will probably gain improved self-confidence and self-image once she learns what is expected of her. After she has progressed successfully through this learning experience you can praise or even reward her with a small gift or treat as a way to show her how proud you are.

For a toddler or preschooler who is no longer in a crib and is perfectly able to come to your room in the middle of the night, explain that she is not allowed to leave her room when it is still dark out. Remind her that unless it is an emergency, it is not polite to wake up people who are sleeping. You may explain this in terms like, "Honey, mommy is a better mommy for you during the day if I am able to sleep all night without an interruption." If she does come to your room in the middle of the night, explain sternly that she is not to come to you unless she is sick or afraid and walk her back to her bed without any talking or playing.

If your child continues to leave her room at night or if she uses the terms "I am sick" or "I am afraid" too often, you should explain to her that if she continues to do what you have asked her not to do that you will have to temporarily lock her room. You can reassure your child you will open the lock as soon as she is quiet and it becomes clear that she plans to stay in her room. You can also install a half door so you can lock the bottom half while leaving the top half open. Keeping your child in her room at night is not cruel. You are being a wise, safe and caring parent by making sure your child is not able to wander around the house at night.

If your child fights bedtime and falls asleep late after a long period of noise and complaints, wake her up at the time in the morning you would like her to awaken. She will likely be more tired the next evening and thus be less energetically resistant to her bedtime routine.

Do not begin this process until you feel able to carry the lesson out completely *without giving in* for the week or so that the training will take. Sometimes parents must teach social rules so that they can maintain their own health, minimize family and marital stressors, or help guide their child toward normal developmental milestones. You can allow a child to awaken the household every night for many years. But this is usually not desirable for the child, the parent, the marriage and family, or for the relationship between the child and parent.

Many parents choose to let their children sleep with them in their room or bed. There is nothing wrong with this choice as long as both parents are honestly okay with this and neither is being forced by the other or the child against his or her wishes. There is no evidence that bed-sharing does any harm to children, nor does it make them more spoiled. In fact, when bed-sharing is genuinely desired by both parents and the child, there is evidence that this can be a good thing for their relationship. *But only if ALL the bed partners desire and want it.* If you have been allowing your child to share your bed with you and then decide that you want to change this, you should understand that he is unlikely to be happy about this and, as we discussed earlier in this section, you are probably going to be in for a difficult week. But this is okay, not at all harmful to your child, and nothing you should feel guilty about.

Remember that being able to demonstrate self-soothing and bedtime autonomy oftentimes provides an exciting and rewarding achievement and feeling of independence for your child.

Ideally, try not to make this change when your child is in the middle of any other serious adjustment (an increase in family stress or tension, a current or recent illness, a recent or impending move, a new baby, etc.). Also make sure that you underscore that this is in no way a form of rejection. Explain what is going to happen when you both have an uninterrupted time to talk during the day. While gazing in his eyes and holding and touching him, tell him that you and Daddy have decided that from now on you need to have time alone in the bedroom during the night. Reassure him that you and Daddy still totally love and adore him and this decision has nothing to do with how much you love him.

Regression—"Acting Like a Baby"

Two- to three-year-olds are the most prone to wanting to relive aspects of their babyhood. When tired they may want to be carried or fed as they were when they were a baby. Young toddlers and preschoolers will also regress when their family life undergoes a significant rise in its stress level. Sometimes a previously potty trained toddler will refuse to use the potty chair, or a child who has previously slept uneventfully through the night will begin night awakenings. This is known as regression. Regression happens as a form of adaptation in response to a child's feeling stressed, unsafe or less secure, and more threatened than previously. It is a defense mechanism and, without it, a child might become totally overwhelmed by the anxiety and could become nearly paralyzed in dealing with his life. Regression makes the stress more manageable and less threatening.

Parents who are prepared for temporary setbacks connected with high stress levels are better able to accept their child's regression without anxiety and are better prepared to allow their children to work out their needs in their own way. When we permit an older toddler or preschooler to talk baby talk, suck on a bottle, or eat like a baby, we are accepting him the way he is right now trusting full well that soon enough he will gather his own resources to regain his previous stage of development. You are their safe harbor—you are their secure base and safe port in a storm. You are the only place they feel safe to revert to some of the old comfortable behaviors that they recall brought them much comfort.

Parents should stay as calm as possible about their child's transient developmental setbacks. Try not to view his behaviors as a failure of your parenting or a reason to feel guilty. Usually, as soon as the family's stressful period abates, your child will return to his previous functioning level.

Sleepwalking

About one in six normal toddlers and preschoolers sleepwalk. You know your child walks in her sleep if she walks while her eyes are open but blank, she is not well-coordinated in her semipurposeful acts (dressing, undressing, opening and closing doors, turning on and off lights, etc.), and is not easily awakened. Sleepwalking is more common in older preschoolers, begins one or two hours after going to sleep, and lasts 5 to 20 minutes. Gently lead your child back to her bed. Fatigue and exhaustion tend to increase the likelihood of sleepwalking. If you need to awaken your child in the morning, this indicates that she needs more sleep—put her to bed earlier in the evening.

Think of your child's sleepwalking as a symptom that she is telling you she needs to have her physical needs for more sleep met or as a symptom that she is feeling distressed about something that happened to her. Think through her day and see if you can help her avoid, or at least lessen, this type of stress. Doing this means you are being a good safe harbor for her and are acting as a parent who is seeking to provide as secure a base as possible for her.

Human beings make strong bonds to others. Attachment behavior is the form of behavior that results in a child's attaining or retaining proximity to her primary caregiver, who is hopefully stronger and wiser so she can feel safe and secure. Whether a child becomes attached in a healthy way depends on your sensitivity in responding to your child's signals *and* the amount and nature of your interaction with your child.

Children are molded by the type of love they receive. A child's experience and relationship with her main caregivers is critical to her psychological development and relates directly to whether her normal developmental problem behaviors are mild and constantly resolving or become intense and stuck. Many forms of intense problem behaviors and psychiatric problems that emerge later in life can be attributed to problems in the development of a child's attachment with his primary caregiver.

The problem behaviors addressed in this chapter are most effectively diminished by utilizing Principle #1. This does not mean that Principles #2 and #3 will not also help in dealing with them—just as a healthy dose of Principle #1 can help with the behaviors discussed in later chapters. Remember the stool—your child needs all three legs (Principles) to be sturdy (happy) and not fall down. But the problem behaviors addressed in this chapter should first be addressed by recalling Principle #1 and attempting to ensure yourself that you are doing everything possible to provide your child with a secure attachment.

CHAPTER 4

Parenting Principle #2: Be a Good Boss

What do you think of when you think of someone who is a "good boss?" That she lets you know what is expected of you and what her rules are? That she makes decisions and exerts authority in a responsible and caring manner? That she praises you for a job well done and offers constructive criticism when necessary? That she is fair and consistent? That she gives you the opportunity for promotions and better compensation for good work? It is essential that parents of toddlers and preschoolers be "good bosses" to their children.

Are you feeling a bit uncomfortable with my choice of the word "boss?" Let me explain. Remember that Principle #2 is one of three essential aspects to our roles as good parents. While Principle #1 describes the love and security aspects of our relationship with our child, Principle #2 meets our children's need for someone to be in charge—someone who is strong and willing to face anger, rebellion and disapproval in a responsible way. Parents must set firm limits and responsibilities and require that their children accept fundamental teaching and rules with respect in order for them to emerge from childhood in a healthy way.

When many people think of discipline, they think in negative terms; images of spanking and punishment come to mind. The word "discipline," however, comes from the word "disciple," and a disciple is someone who follows a teacher. That is what you are: a teacher showing your child how to cooperate with others and deal with the anger and frustrations of life. We must discipline because proper discipline is essential for a child's developing personality. The goal of discipline (from a "good boss") is to instruct, teach, guide, and help children develop their own self-discipline. Structures, limits, and routines help kids develop a sense of predictability and a capacity for self-regulation and self-control. Children feel safe when they feel safely contained within their "good boss's" rules and structures.

We live in an organized society where if a young child has not been taught the rules and requirements of the "life game" early (while still under the love, affection, and tenderness of one's parents), he will be taught them later by strangers (oftentimes by "bad bosses") who couldn't care less if the lessons inflict major harm to his personality and future aspirations. A child must learn that his first teacher in life is correct and can be trusted and obeyed. We must help our child learn early (from a "good boss") to deal appropriately with authority—children who never learn to respect authority find themselves extraordinarily handicapped later in life.

A child cooperates in his life training for two main reasons: (1) because he wants to retain his parents' love and approval and (2) because he wants to maximize his parents' granting of freedoms and favors.

You might wonder, "Why would he need to act in any specific way to retain my love and approval? Aren't I supposed to love my child the same regardless of how he acts?" Actually, no. Parents do not—and should not—feel the same toward their child regardless of whether he gives them an adoring hug and sloppy kiss or kicks them in a furious rage. Human beings don't respond that way, regardless of the relationships involved. This is a fundamental component of the parent/child relationship, because if we felt the same toward our children regardless of their behavior, they would have little motivation to act in a way that society accepts.

Parents have two types of love for their kids: fundamental love and affectionate love. Fundamental love is a forever, solid, unwavering, secure base love that parents hold for their child regardless of how he acts because he is your child. Fundamental love is the foundation of Principle #1. Fundamental love is unconditional and everlasting and your child needs to know that it is always present regardless of how he is acting. You remind your child, through hugs, touch, and eye contact, that though you may at times disapprove of his actions or behaviors, you still love him forever and deeply.

Affectionate love is addressed in Principle #2. We base affectionate love upon how we feel about our child's actions. This is, in fact, a conditional love, and parents do not need to feel guilty about this. A child needs to know that his parents do not feel the same affection toward him regardless of his actions. Affectionate love requires reciprocal behaviors from your child. He cannot expect you to remain affectionate when he acts unlovingly or disrespectfully toward you. This, of course, is not to suggest that you should ever do anything to make your child feel utterly unloved and abandoned, and it is of the utmost importance that you demonstrate your affectionate love as soon as your child's behaviors warrant the return of good feelings. Explain this to your child, even at a very early age. Let him know that you will always love him and be available to him (i.e., "fundamental love"), but that he sometimes makes you angry and frustrated and that you will let him know when this occurs.

Securely attached children desperately want the approval of their parents. This is a good and necessary thing. Because they feel emotionally tied to their parents, when a parent temporarily withholds approval and affection, the child feels a number of emotional reactions about himself that combine to create a feeling of guilt. This is not the unhealthy guilt that causes a child to feel deep shame. It is a healthy guilt essential to his developing a fully working conscience.

Understanding the two types of love and the importance of temporarily withholding affection, favors, and approval is the foundation to being a good boss and mastering Principle #2.

How Soon Can I Start to Discipline?

By the age of nine months, your baby is smarter than almost every other creature on earth. Before she is a year old, she is more intelligent than the family dog, and the dog is fully capable of learning to "sit," "stay," and "come here." Even if your child has a very limited vocabulary, she can still understand disciplinary actions that include absolutely no words. For example, if your child throws her bottle and you are tired of retrieving it, merely remove it. If she won't sit in her high chair, fasten the seat belt. If she purposely spits out her carrots, just take the food away.

You can begin to discipline with words not long after this. A healthy toddler understands most verbal disciplinary instructions by 18 months and has a fully functioning memory by age two. Her verbal achievements may limit her ability to respond, but if you *expect understanding* from your child and speak to her in a manner that inspires respect, this interaction will promote healthy growth throughout her childhood.

One caution: avoid disciplining in matters you cannot enforce without your child's decision to follow your command. For example, a parent cannot force a child to swallow, eat, sleep, and so on.

Each time you attempt a lesson that you cannot enforce, you undermine your authority and suggest to your child that her teacher is not dependable. Therefore, commanding your child to "eat your food," "go to sleep," "poop in the potty," "stop crying," or anything of this sort undermines your position as a "good boss" if your child doesn't comply. Instead, make statements that *are* enforceable: "the meal is over in five minutes," "you need to stay in your bedroom and I'll see you in the morning," "as soon as you poop in the potty we can go play in the park," "looks like you need a 'time out' until you stop crying," and so on.

As your child becomes a toddler, you have an obligation to teach her about the realities of the world regardless of whether she wants to learn these things. Safety is a top concern. You can never allow your young child to decide any issues that threaten her safety. She needs to learn that when her "good boss" declares something is unsafe, she must obey. If an activity runs a risk of seriously injuring or harming her, you must let her know—through firm holding, firm words, firm redirection, and firm expressions—that under no circumstances will you allow her to come into harm's way. Limit your child physically when necessary. Let her know that there is absolutely no wiggle room for her misbehavior when it comes to her safety.

There is another category regarding safety issues, however. If you determine that an activity is unwise but will not seriously harm or injure your child, it is best for you to warn her of the danger but allow her to learn on her own. For example, you may say something like, "Johnny, if you stand on the step stool that way you may fall off and bump yourself" or, "Erin, if you don't let mommy tie your shoelaces you may trip and fall on the grass." Then back off and see what happens. When your child experiments with not listening to you, a certain amount of very mild discomfort will help her realize what a wise and good boss you are. Showing what a good boss you are is better than the alternative.

Parents who hover over their kids to try and avoid all painful falls or spills will often create children who are either oblivious to how to keep themselves safe, or who become risk takers because they are sick of parents who act like helicopters over them.

Don't overwarn. If you do, you run the risk of turning this lesson into a battle of wills. Simply tell her while making direct eye contact and then back off. Some of the time, nothing will happen. She won't fall off the chair or trip. This is fine. The lesson will come later. If, however, your child doesn't listen to you and is slightly hurt because of this, offer her empathy and comfort while gently reminding her that you cautioned her. "Ooh, I'm sorry you fell off the step stool. I'll bet that hurts. Mommy warned you that might happen." "Oh, honey, I'll bet that feels awful. Next time maybe you'll want Mommy to tie your shoelaces." Don't gloat and don't overdiscuss it; allow the natural consequences of her not listening to your warnings to sink in. Talking too much about it makes a child defensive and causes her to miss the message

The third category of problem behaviors includes those unrelated to safety issues. This category is by far the largest of the three and the one that most often confounds parents regarding discipline.

A Good Boss Knows When to Give and When to Take Away Goodies

Let's go back to the analogy we've been working with in this chapter. A good boss sets limits and establishes the rules. A good boss also lays out our job responsibilities and rewards us (through money, promotions, acknowledgment) when we perform them well and withholds these rewards when we don't. An employer/employee relationship involves the doling out of "goodies" for good performance. A healthy parent/child relationship operates in much the same way.

Here's the most important phrase related to Principle #2: "Show me the goods and you'll get your goodies." Indeed, like any good boss, you need to engage in an ongoing series of transactions with your child if you are going to get the best behavior from him. Are you thinking to yourself "Is this really necessary? Shouldn't good behavior be based on doing something because it is correct, not because a child is rewarded for it?" You may be wondering why your child can't "be good for goodness' sake." Doing the right thing just because it is the right thing to do is certainly a lovely ideal. The problem is that this motivation for behavior is one that gradually develops over one's entire childhood and adolescence. In fact, as adults there are still many behaviors ("goods") we choose to do primarily because there are rewards ("goodies") or consequences ("lack of goodies") attached to the behavior. For example, adults may choose to work hard to receive a good paycheck or raise, to follow social decorum to obtain social benefits, or to obey laws to avoid legal problems.

What are "the goods" that apply to children? These are specific behavioral expectations you will hold your child to depending on his developmental age and his physical and mental capabilities. These expectations include:

❏ **RESPECT.** Does your child show an age appropriate evidence of respect for you and other adults in his life? Did three-year-old Suzy look in Grandma's eyes and thank her for the cookie (even if you had to remind her gently)? After an adequate number of reminders, did she remember to say "thank you" on her own? Did four-year-old Johnny listen carefully as you talked with him about his behavior instead of rolling his eyes and looking off into the distance?

❏ **ABILITY.** Does your child show an age appropriate ability to handle circumstances and responsibilities? Did four-year-old Jim show the ability to put his emotions into words by telling you that he was feeling mad, sad, or bad? When two-year-old Anne removed everything from her bedroom drawer, did she show patience and work hard to help you put everything back after her "time out?"

❏ **GOOD JUDGMENT.** Does your child show you an age appropriate ability to make good choices? Does four-year-old Sally show proper judgment in obeying the safety rules you've explained to her? Did three-year-old Kay accept your explanation of why she couldn't wear her bathing suit to church instead of having a tantrum before complying?

❏ **SELF-CONTROL.** Was five-year-old Steven able to calm down and talk about his emotions after screaming at you when you insisted he get ready for school? Did two-year-old Marge stop chasing and scaring the dog and instead accept your guidance in petting his fur gently?

If your child is showing you these "goods," he is in line to receive "goodies." "Goodies" are age appropriate freedoms and favors. For toddlers and preschoolers, these include extra attention, praise, approval, gifts, and the freedom to make personal choices about their lifestyles. For example, the "goodies" for children this age might include such things as an extra board game you might play with him, a small "sweet treat," the addition of a type of TV program he previously couldn't watch, or the freedom to pick out his own clothing.

The "goodies" you grant your child are linked to the degree to which your child has shown you "the goods" for the past minute, hour, or day (depending on his ability and age). The process of granting or removing "goodies" based upon your child's demonstration of "the goods" is a continual fluid process. If "the goods" are in constant evidence, you might want to increase the number of "goodies" you offer. On the other hand, if your child lapses in showing you "the goods," you will want to appropriately lessen or take back one or more of his "goodies."

Even young toddlers are able to learn how their behaviors over the past hour or so link to the "goodies" they receive. The younger the child, the closer the link needs to be. For example, if your two-year-old child wants a cookie, you might say, "Honey, a few minutes ago, you didn't show me the goods when you kept chasing the cat even after I asked you to stop. Maybe if you show me the goods by not scaring the cat until lunch you can get your goodie after that." Two- and three-year-old children should be able to understand this link even after a few hours have passed. Four- and five-year-old children can understand the link between "goods" and "goodies" even after a day or more. For example, a five-year-old child might ask to have a play date and your response might be, "I'd love to allow you to go and play this afternoon, but you didn't show me the goods this morning when you left your toys all over the floor after I asked you to pick them up. Maybe if you show me the goods by cleaning up now, you can have a play date tomorrow."

If you decide that your child will not be receiving a "goodie" because he hasn't shown you "the goods," explain it fully (how his inability to demonstrate good behavior has led to his not being awarded a freedom or favor) and then *stop talking and stay neutral and calm.* The explanation should include an example of how the behavior failed to show respect, ability, good judgment and/or self-control ("You didn't show Mommy respect when you ignored something I asked you to do.") and how this has resulted in the "goodie" being withheld. That's it. Further explanations, criticism, or emphasis on his mistakes hinders your child's ability to think and grow. By being concise, you allow the impact of what you just said to sink in.

Your ability to control your child's behavior comes from your power over him to remove or not grant him "goodies." If somehow this doesn't appear to have an immediate impact, don't worry. If keeping away this particular "goodie" wasn't motivating enough, you will have plenty of additional opportunities to reinforce this point at other junctures.

Here's an example of how this works. Four-year-old Tommy didn't listen to his father Joe when he asked him to stay out of a muddy puddle while wearing his church clothes. On his way to church, he asked to play with his Game Boy and his father said, "Honey, I'd like to be able to let you do that, but you didn't show me the goods earlier. You didn't use your self-control when you jumped in the puddle after I asked you not to. I'm going to have to keep the Game Boy up in the front seat with me. Maybe if you keep your new clothes clean until we get home, you can get a goodie later." After church, Joe reminded him to stay clean while he talked to friends for a few minutes. Instead, he slid down a banister and landed in a thorny bush, dirtying and tearing his jacket. Joe stayed calm, but on the way home, he said, "Tommy, I guess not being able to play with your video game wasn't enough of a goodie to take away to remind you that you need to show me the goods. You didn't show me respect, ability, good judgment, or self-control when you got dirty again. When we get home, instead of having the play date we set up, you will help me wash the clothes and fix your jacket."

When your child wants more freedom or favors than you think he is ready to receive, tell him in a way that lets him know you understand his discomfort with a decision you've made in his best interests. For example, "I see that you are upset that you can't stay up later, but right now your bedtime is 8:00." Your comfort with his anger at you will confirm that he has a "good boss" willing to make good decisions even in the face of an angry response. This makes him feel safe.

At the same time, if you feel your child has shown a level of respect, ability, good judgment, and self-control to warrant an expansion of his freedoms, make sure you let him understand that you are doing this because he has shown you "the goods." "You've really shown us the goods at bedtime by getting ready for bed quickly and not giving us a hard time when it's time to go upstairs. Because of this, Mommy and Daddy have decided that your new bedtime is 8:15. Great going—you have shown really good respect, ability, good judgment, and self-control about bedtime."

Does all of this sound like behavior modification? In fact, it is. *But life works that way.* The lack of respect, ability, good judgment, and self-control can lead to safety risks, failure in school, poor job performance, and even trouble with the law when your child gets older. You are being a "good boss" if you discipline with a method that endorses and supports the realities of life.

The Four Components of Being a Good Boss

When your child breaks a rule, she needs to understand that you disapprove of what she has done. Remember to contain your comments to the act and not the child. There is a mountain of difference between the following two comments:

"You are a bad girl for kicking me in the shins."

"Kicking me in the shins is very bad, and I won't tolerate it."

It is relatively harmless to let a child know that her actions are unacceptable and even deplorable. On the other hand, you can do enormous damage to her self-image if you suggest to her that her *very being* is at fault.

When tensions and emotions run high, make sure to adopt the four components of being a good boss:

❏ **VERBALLY EXPRESS YOUR OWN EMOTIONS.** When your child has broken a rule, express your anger in a nonphysical and noninsulting way. "You didn't listen to Daddy and that makes me very angry." "You threw and broke my favorite dish and that makes Mommy sad and want to cry." When people express their feelings, the feelings diminish in intensity. How you model your anger will help your child tremendously. Remember, kids learn the most through imitating their parents.

Keep your initial response to an expression of your intense feeling. Saying anything more almost always leads to blaming, shaming, threatening, abandoning, pleading, weakness, bargaining, aggression, or deferring to a higher authority. None of these help your child and will lead him to lose respect for your authority as a "good boss." Avoid saying things like:

➤ "You've ruined my day. I don't know what to do with you." (Blaming)

➤ "What a naughty bad little boy you are to do that." (Shaming)

➤ "Don't you dare get angry with me or I'll show you what real anger is." (Threatening)

➤ "Get out of my sight. You do that again, and I'll leave you here." (Abandoning)

➤ "Can't you do this one thing for me? Can't you help me out here?" (Pleading)

➤ "OK, I give up. Have it your way." (Weakness)

➤ "If you do this now, I'll give you a treat later." (Bargaining)

➤ "I know what's best for you, so just shut up and do as I say." (Aggression)

➤ "The police will get you for this." (Deferring to a higher authority)

❑ **NEVER GIVE CONSEQUENCES IN THE HEAT OF BATTLE.** Consequences given under these circumstances are rarely the best ones. Here's an example. Four-year-old Jenny was a notorious dawdler. The more her mother Susan scolded, pressured, reasoned, or begged her to hurry, the more she slowed down. One day Susan called from the next room, "Jenny, Mommy *really* needs to get to the doctor's office on time today. I need you to get your shoes and coat on and be ready to be at the front door right away." After Jenny responded, "Okay," Susan rushed around and finally reached the front door only to discover that Jenny was not there. Susan ran around the house frantically and finally located Jenny sitting on the basement floor playing with dolls. Furious, Susan screamed, "Okay, that does it. I've had it with you. You can't go to the birthday party this afternoon."

What will undoubtedly happen here? Jenny, realizing that she pushed her mother too far, will either spend the next few hours pleading with Susan to change her mind or will be terrifically sweet and compliant in the hopes that she'll get her way. In the meantime, Susan will calm down, realize that her punishment was too harsh, and relent, letting Jenny go to the party. Unfortunately, the message Jenny hears in this is that she doesn't need to listen to her mother until her mother explodes and even then, the explosion doesn't matter much because her mother doesn't follow through on her threats. She might even get the impression that she has the upper hand in the relationship because regardless of what she does, there are few consequences.

Let's replay this scenario a different way. Susan sees Jenny playing on the floor. Susan almost loses it because she really needed Jenny to come through for her this time, but in spite of her internal rage, all she says is, "Jenny, Mommy is very angry at you right now. You really didn't show me the goods by ignoring me, so I'm going to take away goodies. I'll let you know later what I decide."

Later in the day, a calmed Susan says to Jenny, "Jenny, Mommy gets very upset when you don't listen. You didn't show me respect when you ignored me. Since you didn't show me the goods, you lose goodies. Mommy has decided that after the party until bedtime you will stay near me and help me with my chores instead of watching any TV." This is a much, much more successful approach. Jenny has once again had the expectations of "goods for goodies" explained and interpreted for her. She learns that her mom takes the time to think clearly about her behavior and carries through on what she says she'll do. She learns that her mother is a "good boss."

❏ **DISENGAGE WITH A ONE-LINER.** If your anger doesn't go away by expressing it, then learn a "one-liner" to give you time to calm down. These phrases give you more time and prevent you from having a harmful dialogue with your child. For example, Tommy knew how to frustrate his parents. As a verbally gifted four-year-old, he knew exactly what buttons to push when facing consequences for his behavior. He has retorts at his disposal like, "You didn't do this to Sam when he was bad; that must mean you don't love me" or "I told Johnny he could see my toy when he came over; what am I going to do now that you took it away?" or "Daddy wouldn't do something like this."

Tommy's mother will probably be tempted to respond to these comments in some way. Instead of entering into the fray, though, she would be better off repeating her "one-liner" over and over to everything Tommy said. Saying something like "nice try" keeps her in control and allows her to maintain her position as a "good boss."

Your favorite "one-liner" should be as neutral as possible and not something that your child can interpret as denigrating. Here are some options:

➤ Nice try.

➤ I'll get back to you on that.

➤ I'll let you know.

➤ That's sad, but I still love you.

➤ We'll talk about it later.

➤ Learning about life is a challenge.

➤ You'll figure it out.

❑ **USE A "TIME OUT" TO LESSEN TENSIONS AND EMOTIONS.** A "time out" can be very effective for toddlers and preschoolers when you need to make them understand their behavior is unacceptable. It works well for children from 18 months to six years and is particularly useful for temper tantrums, whining, yelling, fighting, and aggressive behavior. Your first option (using Principle #1) is to have your child stay beside you as you remain completely neutral and calm. Honestly, though, are you able to take him in your arms and hold him through his crying and screaming without feeling "triggered?"

If your child is seriously out of control or if you believe it is better for your own emotional state to have him express his strong emotions away from you, then you must guide him (with a minimum of force) to a "think-it-over spot." This should be a safe place devoid of anything that will entertain him or that he can break or destroy. Some kids need a special contained space away from everyone to calm down. Others are fine with a special chair that prevents them from seeing anything else going on in the room.

If your child needs a special contained place away from others, lead him there and then ask him if he needs you to leave the door open or closed. If he doesn't answer or answers "open" and stays in the room, you can leave the door open. If he attempts to leave the room before you are ready to allow him out, then you will need to have a way to contain him in the room safely and easily. Stay just outside the door (without letting him know it) to make sure he stays safe—this way you will be ready to enter the room when he is ready to talk with you.

When you use a "time out," remember that children want positive attention from their parents. When they can't have positive attention, they will settle for negative attention. What they *never* want is to be ignored. This is why "time out" works after repeated use. Kids think to themselves, "Wow, this obviously isn't too successful. When I do this Mommy puts me in 'time out' and I don't get *any* attention from her. I guess I'll find another way to get her to pay attention to me." "Time out" works particularly well for those children who receive lots of attention when they are behaving normally. If a child doesn't receive much attention from their parents when he or she is being good, "time out" doesn't have the same impact.

How long should your child stay in "time out?" Many parenting books suggest it should last approximately one minute per year of age. Arbitrary periods are problematic, however, because they do not reward your child for getting his emotions under control faster and the extra time alone in his "think-it-over spot" does nothing positive for your child. Additionally, toddlers and preschoolers should be required to share what they have learned about the behavior that put them in "time out" in the first place.

The following guideline is the best approach for your child because he learns self-control and how to make amends for misbehavior:

➤ Make it clear you will not remove him from "time out" until he quiets and calms himself down. Be patient. For some kids, their first few experiences in "time out" are lengthy.

➤ After your child is quiet, tell him that before he can leave "time out" he must apologize and make amends. When your child apologizes (even if you need to prompt his response), you can respond with a hug and kiss and an acknowledging statement that puts his misbehavior into perspective: "Honey, I accept your apology. I love you. Sometimes it takes being away from people to be able to control your emotions."

Your child should also understand that there are a number of ways he can "fix things" to your satisfaction. If nothing is broken, a big hug might be the answer. You can talk briefly about how he could handle his anger better next time. If something broke or if another's feelings got hurt, you can help him think of ways to make amends for this, for example helping to clean up or apologizing to the person whose feelings he hurt.

A Few Words about Spanking

Most parents struggle over spanking, perhaps more than any other parenting issue. This topic brings out the most contentious, angry, and defensive reactions from parents and those who have justified spanking in their own minds oftentimes become defensive or embarrassed about it.

There are pros and cons to spanking. Spanking in this context refers only to the use of an open hand to strike a child on the buttocks or extremities with the intention of altering or stopping the child's behavior without causing physical injury. You should *never use* other types of physical punishment (using an object, striking a child in other places on his body or face, hitting with a force that causes a mark that lasts more than a few minutes, shaking, pinching, pulling or jerking a child's body part). This kind of punishment runs the risk of inflicting permanent injury and could get the parent in trouble with the law. See Chapter 10 if you are unable to stop yourself from using these other forms of physical force on your child.

The pros to spanking are:

❏ **SPANKING CAN IMMEDIATELY REDUCE OR** stop an unwanted behavior if used extremely infrequently in selective circumstances (for instance when the child's behavior is so unsafe or dangerous that he could be significantly or permanently harmed).

❏ **IT IS POSSIBLY NOT HARMFUL** if fully accepted within a person's culture, ethnicity, class, or religious affiliation and is done only occasionally by loving parents who give reasons for their actions.

The cons to spanking are:

❏ **THOUGH SPANKING MAY IMMEDIATELY STOP** a behavior, if used as a primary discipline method, it can only retain effectiveness with increased intensity. This requires greater and greater force until the parent runs the risk of delivering a spanking of such intensity that society considers it abuse.

❏ **SPANKING MODELS AN AGGRESSIVE BEHAVIOR** as a way to deal with conflicts. Research shows that preschoolers who are spanked show a much higher rate of aggressive behaviors. When an older child or adolescent is spanked consistently, he is statistically far more likely to have depression or anxiety disorders or to be a substance abuser, or criminal, or lead a violent life as an adult.

❏ **MOST PARENTS DESCRIBE SPANKING AS** a form of discipline. By definition then, spanking should teach a lesson or correct a behavior. The problem is that a spanked child may feel that his spanking "canceled" his crime thus leaving him free to recommit the offense.

❏ **SPANKING ALLOWS A CHILD TO** think that physical aggression is an acceptable and effective way to solve problems and allows a child to focus on his or her grievance rather than on his or her own misbehavior and the harm it may have caused to others.

❏ **THE CHILD CAN KEEP A** "sin" ledger where a spanking wipes his slate clean thus allowing him to avoid the healthy guilt feelings that help a person strive to behave in ways that avoid this temporary personal discomfort.

❏ **IF SPANKING IS USED LIBERALLY** when a child is younger, the parent-child relationship becomes centered on power issues; this makes disciplining an older child virtually impossible when spanking is no longer an option.

❏ **SPANKING CAN BECOME ADDICTIVE BECAUSE** it affords a parent brief relief from anger.

❏ **RESEARCH SHOWS THAT THE MORE** a child is spanked the more likely it is that he will be involved in spouse or child abuse when he is an adult.

After a spanking, kids tend to think one or more of the following four "R's":

❏ Resentment ("I hate him for doing that").

❏ Revenge ("She got me now but I'll get even later").

❑ Rebellion ("I'll still do what I want but I'll just be more careful and not get caught next time").

❑ Reduced self-esteem ("I must be a horrible person to be hit and humiliated like this—I guess I'm not a good person").

In addition, children who are spanked tend to view adults as frightening and unpredictable.

I look at spanking this way: if your intent is not to spank, you will probably spank about the right amount. If you occasionally spank when you are acting from an unplanned basic human reaction to an overwhelming emotion and you handle the aftermath appropriately, then there is probably no harm done whatsoever.

So what is the best way to handle the situation after you spank? First, you need to forgive yourself because there is no shame in being human. We *all* lose it from time to time. Then you need to complete the lesson for your child. If you feel so angry or guilty that you can't talk about what happened for a while, tell your child the truth. Then, after you regain your composure and calm down, you need to share a "corrective apology" by saying something like this: "A few minutes ago I was so terribly angry with what you did that I spanked you because I lost control of my emotions. This doesn't make what I did right, and I'm sorry. It doesn't make what *you* did right though, either. You were wrong to (run into the street, hit me, etc.), and you must never do this again." Such an admission teaches the child that even his powerful parents make and admit their mistakes and apologize. Something good can come from something that is probably best avoided.

Being a "good boss" takes hard work and diligence. By mastering Principle #2, though, you can navigate through any number of difficult situations with your child and, more importantly, teach him valuable lessons about how the world works and how to succeed in that world.

In addition to hard work and diligence, Principle #2 requires a consistency and "stick-to-itiveness." If your child is living with both of his parents in the same household, then it is important that Principle #2 be consistently applied by both parents. Some parents function well when one parent takes the lead in doling out or limiting the "goodies" in response to the child's behaviorally demonstrated "goods" with the other parent supporting and following this lead. Other parents function well when they agree privately ahead of time what "goods" they expect and what the limitation or awarding of the "goodies" will be. In any case, parents in the same household must agree and be consistent. Undermining the other parent's decisions can have disastrous consequences because the child is not being raised by "good bosses." Parents who cannot get "on the same page" should seek outside counsel. For additional thoughts, read the section on Parenting in the Face of Bitter Parental Fighting, Separation or Divorce in Chapter 9.

The next chapter looks at specific problem behaviors and shows you how the effective use of Principle #2 can help you to deal with them.

CHAPTER 5

Putting Principle #2 to Work

Children whose parents are good bosses understand the necessary limits society puts on them and how increased favors and privileges are rewards for good behavior. The problem behaviors discussed in this chapter occur when children aren't sufficiently schooled in the concept of "goods for goodies" and therefore fail to see their parents as "good bosses." While Principle #1 and Principle #3 will help with these behaviors, look first to Principle #2 when dealing with these issues.

Always keep in mind that the system of "goods for goodies" requires time and patience. If your child seems to repeat his bad behaviors, stay the course and stick to the system. Parenting requires an almost infinite amount of patience to help your child master self-control. Learning how to "show the goods" is an ongoing process that takes a long time—virtually your child's entire childhood. Don't try to rush the learning process by expecting too much. Look for a steady improvement, even if progress seems incredibly slow. Keep a diary if that helps you keep track of things. You might find it useful to see how your child's difficult behaviors change from month to month and this can reinforce that you are indeed making progress.

The problem behaviors covered in this chapter are:

❏ Anger and defiance

❏ Bullying and aggression

❏ Fighting with siblings

❏ Hitting, biting, and scratching

❏ Jealousy and not sharing

❏ Not listening, stubbornness, and willfulness

❏ Rudeness and disrespect

❏ "Sassy" and "mouthy" behavior

❏ Tattling

❏ Temper tantrums

Anger and Defiance

The research is very clear about aggressive behaviors: if a parent addresses these in a two-or-three-year-old with violence, with insults, or by ignoring the behavior, the child is far more likely to exhibit very difficult aggressive behaviors by the age of four. This is most particularly true if your child is a boy. It is therefore essential that you handle these situations the right way as early as possible.

Children show aggressive behaviors most often when they are angry. The first and most basic cause of profound anger comes from disruptions in the attachment relationship between the primary care provider and the child (as discussed in Principle #1). Under these circumstances, almost every part of a child's identity, self-worth, and emotional base emanates from anger. In such a state, toddlers and preschoolers may redirect their anger into aggression toward other targets, such as peers or siblings. Perpetually angry young children are often a signal to a family that the family as a whole is holding a lot of anger. Parents who think of their child as "always bad" or "always angry" should look at their family situation. By looking within yourself and your spouse, you may find ways to make necessary adjustments. We will cover this in much more detail in Chapter 10.

When your child acts angry or aggressively, first take a look at his life to determine if he needs more of Principle #1 to feel safe and secure. If you feel his anger is not the result of severe attachment trauma, move to the "goods for goodies" method. If this doesn't work at first, this means he needs even fewer freedoms or favors so he will be motivated to gain the necessary self-control. Sometimes keeping your child close to you nonstop works miraculously because it makes him feel more contained and held and thus more secure and less angry. Add goodies as long as his anger is absent and restrict these goodies if his anger returns.

Sometimes it works to have your child practice how to act when he gets angry. For example, four-year-old Timmy had trouble with his anger when he didn't get his way. His mom picked a time when he was not in this state and said, "Honey, I've noticed that sometimes when I tell you that you can't do something you get very angry with me." Timmy nodded. His mother continued, "Would you like me to help you show me the goods." Timmy nodded again. "Well, Honey, if you feel a mad feeling coming, I want you to play a game where you pretend you are blowing out a hundred candles on a huge cake. Pretend that it takes you many, many breaths to blow them all out and you have to take deep, deep breaths to get enough air." They practiced this for a while and then his mom said, "Now pretend you just asked me if you could go play with Johnny and I said you couldn't. Pretend you are really mad at me. What would you do?" She watched as he practiced, then said, "If I can see the 'mad' coming, do you want me to remind you by saying the words, 'candles on a cake'?" Timmy nodded and she began to use this method whenever she saw his anger bubbling up. You can use this or some variation, such as punching a pillow or a punching bag—anything that is physical, won't hurt your child or others, and employs large muscles.

Kids will sometimes get so angry that they threaten to run away from home. What they are really saying when they make this threat is: "Do you love me enough to keep me from leaving you even when I am angry at you?" Children desperately want to believe that no matter how angry they get, you will still love them and that you are wise enough to set limits on their rash behaviors and will never let them go until they are fully grown up. Parents should respond to their running-away threats with three messages:

❏ "I want to hear more about why you are so angry."

❏ "It's perfectly natural to sometimes feel uncontrollably angry at me and I accept those feelings in you."

❏ "I don't want you to leave because I love you and I want you to stay with me."

Bullying and Aggression

Some degree of aggression is natural in toddlers and preschoolers as they develop a sense of themselves, learn how to handle their budding emotions, and learn that their identification with action figures does not allow them to copy these same aggressive actions within society. Some toddlers and preschoolers have a biological tendency to be more aggressive than others. Biologically aggressive two-year-olds often use their physical prowess to get an object or toy they want; biologically aggressive three-year-olds tend to use their words to intimidate others; and biologically aggressive four-to-six-year-olds may demand their way even when there isn't a specific object they desire.

Many studies have shown that aggressive children come from homes where the parents use hostility against each other, where parents discipline with violence, and/or where the parent-child relationship is filled with rejection (rather than using Principle #1). Remember that children learn how to behave in three ways: by copying you, by copying you, and by copying you. If you show aggressive behavior to get your way, your child will likely use this outside of the home.

Young children must be taught the difference between healthy assertiveness and unhealthy aggression, taking the rights and feelings of others into consideration. The "goods for goodies" method is extremely effective at helping your child deal with this. Be careful, though, to keep from sabotaging yourself and the effectiveness of this method. Remember to avoid:

❑ Removing or denying a freedom or favor to "get even" instead of designing one to help the child learn about life and consequences.

❑ Feeling sorry for your child during his "time out" and giving in.

❑ Talking too much about why you have decided to remove or deny a freedom or favor.

❑ Moralizing or threatening, or saying, "This hurts me more than you."

❑ Pleading or acting sarcastic or angry as you tell your child what freedom or favor he has lost.

One note: rarely, some young children have an endocrine hormone abnormality that can cause them to have aggressive behaviors for no apparent reason. Children with this endocrine abnormality are often tall and overly mature for their age (for example, they have large penises, pubic hair, or might masturbate frequently). If you suspect this might be the cause of your child's unexplained angry aggressive outbursts take him to your healthcare provider for a full hormone evaluation.

Fighting with Siblings

Think of the word "sibling" and the word that almost immediately comes to mind is "rivalry." Siblings rarely choose to have each other, and they are forced to share the two people (their parents) they most want solely and exclusively for themselves. They love and bond with each other when they struggle against the rules of their parents. They love each other when they share the fun times of childhood, or when they are protecting each other against bullies in the neighborhood. Yet they also hate each other when their different temperaments cause them to butt heads in the inevitable clashes among family members and when they feel they aren't getting as much attention or goodies from their parents.

All siblings fight when they live in a household with one or more functional parents. In fact, siblings who don't fight are usually being reared in a home where they view their safety and survival as dependent upon joining forces. So view the sibling fights as a compliment to being viewed as a competent parent(s) by your children.

Research shows that 60 to 70 percent of families with children under the ago of six have *at least* one intense physical fight per year among the kids. Whether the fighting gets worse or diminishes as they grow older depends on how parents deal with the fights. Here are some important tips on how *not* to handle sibling fights:

❏ **DON'T INTERFERE IN VERBAL BICKERING.** Parents who give the message that they are the final decision-makers for sibling squabbles end up with children who are too reliant and dependent on them for everything. This invariably results in a rise in sibling hostility.

❏ **DON'T THINK IT IS YOUR** role to find the underlying cause of a conflict between your children. You will rarely be able to find out who did what to whom with any accuracy.

❏ **DON'T ALLOW YOURSELF TO BE** drawn into the fray. You will find yourself using up precious energy and will rarely feel good about your attempt to straighten out the disagreements. Every child longs to hear, "Yes, Jim, you were right and your sister was wrong. Jane obviously started this and I understand why you hit her." Your sending this message is not good for either child.

❏ **DON'T ACT AS A REFEREE** any more than necessary. Step in only if you suspect or fear serious bodily injury of one child toward another.

❏ **DON'T COMPLAIN LOUDLY IN THE** presence of your kids that, "you guys fight all the time." Remember that kids are ready and eager to live up to the expectations and descriptions their parents have of them—particularly when the message is a negative one.

❏ **DON'T ASK YOUR CHILDREN UNANSWERABLE** questions like, "Why can't you be nicer to your sister?" and "Why do you fight so much?"

❏ **DON'T ALLOW YOUR KIDS TO** play one parent against the other. One parent is almost always a little more lenient than the other—and this is usually a healthy thing for kids to experience as long as the parents work out any and all disagreements out of earshot of the kids and present a united supportive front.

Here are the tips on how best to handle sibling fights:

❏ **TELL YOUR KIDS TO WORK** out their differences outside of your earshot. In general, give your kids a "not here" message. Show them that, except in very unusual circumstances, you do not intend to become involved in their squabbles and that you have confidence they can work things out. The more you stay out of the struggle the more ingenious and self-reliant your kids will be in learning to settle their own squabbles.

❏ **IF THE BICKERING SEEMS TO** heat up where you fear one child may injure the other, describe what you see, spell out the limits, and separate the kids if necessary. Say something like, "Whoa, I see two boys who are about to hit each other. Hitting is not allowed in our home. If you can't cool off and talk about it, you will need to go to separate areas of the house."

❏ **IF THERE IS AN INJURY** in a fight, never give your attention to the aggressive child ("Why did you bite him?"). Instead, focus on the injury rather than the fight ("Oh, honey, yes, I see the bite marks. That must hurt. Here, let's go put a cold compress on that."). Talk privately later with the child who delivered the injury; make it clear that you will never tolerate physical violence against another family member (see section below).

❏ **IN AN UNEQUAL CONTEST** (where one sibling is older, stronger, or less vulnerable), the weak usually lose. In situations of inequality where you observe that the stronger one is truly taking advantage of his power, you may have to take the more powerful one aside and let him know in no uncertain terms that, whatever the reasons for his feelings, you expect him to show you the goods in the way he treats his sibling.

❑ **DON'T ASSIGN YOUR CHILDREN THE** roles of prey or aggressor. When you say something like, "Stop doing that, Jimmy, you are scaring her," you give Jimmy a message that you view him as an aggressor with the power to scare his sister and you give your daughter the message that she is too weak to stand up for herself. Remember that our kids live up to the expectations we assign them. Instead, try saying something that will help the "weaker one" view herself in a stronger light while diverting the conflict like, "I'll bet you both can show scary faces. Show me your scariest faces and then let's show Daddy."

Siblings fight, *so get used to it.* Your kids must accept the reality that you do not ever intend to choose one over the other and rid yourself of his unfortunate rival. Once this happens, the hostilities will die down and your kids will find themselves bound together by the common love they have for their parents.

Hitting, Biting, and Scratching

Hitting, biting, and scratching others is a tool toddlers use to try to get what they want. The hitting/biting/scratching stage often occurs when your child is two or three years old. Although this section focuses on "biting" as an example, the advice applies to any form of physical violence from your child.

The biting toddler feels out of control with his anger because he is not getting what he wants. She doesn't necessarily want to hurt anyone, but she doesn't know what to do with her pent-up anger and frustration. Biting makes her feel temporarily better and insures that she'll get a reaction.

Many parents are appalled when they see this kind of action from their child and the temptation is to respond physically—spanking her, washing her mouth out with soap, or even biting her back to "show her how it feels." The problem with these physical reactions is that they send the message that adults can also be irrational and out-of-control when faced with a frustrating situation. Your child really needs a grown-up response that will make him understand that he has a good boss in charge of his irrational acts. Remember, children want limits so they feel contained and held.

When a biting incident occurs, it is important to restrain your child from repeating the behavior. You may need to pick her up and carry her to an isolated place away from others. Tell her very firmly, "No, you must never bite!" Follow this firm command with something like, "Biting is wrong. Biting hurts others and I will not let you bite someone else no matter how angry you feel. Until you feel calmer and in control, you will sit here next to me." It is just as effective to have your child sit alone in her "time out" place if you are too angry to sit next to her.

When she is back in control, ask if she understands that biting is wrong and that you will not tolerate this behavior. Ask for an apology and an admission that what she did was wrong and that she will try not to ever bite again. If she is still angry and will not make this admission, tell her you will come back later to see if she has changed her mind. Repeat this until she relents and then hug her and say something like, "I love you and know you don't want to hurt others. Now you can go back and play, but *don't bite*. If you feel really angry, you may scream, but don't bite."

Jealousy and Not Sharing

For kids, jealousy is one of the base human emotions that appear when there is more than one child in the family. It is important to understand that jealousy among siblings is a forever and powerful force that is always present. About the only time jealousy disappears from siblings is when the parents are gone or not available for a broad variety of reasons (death, absence, dysfunction, sickness, etc.).

If you don't understand why your first-born child might feel jealous when a new baby comes along, imagine coming home one night to find your wife wrapped in the arms of another man. She says to you, "Oh, darling, you have made me so thrilled with having a husband that I have decided to bring home another husband. I just know you will love him. You can help me take care of him. It will be great fun for you to have another husband; you guys will be the best of friends your whole life." Doesn't sound so good, huh?

First-born children have the most trouble with feeling displaced and jealous of the newcomer. How can you expect a child who has had the undivided attention of his parents to enjoy being bumped from his primary position? The goal is to help your first-born feel as little jealousy as is reasonably possible. He should be allowed to grow accustomed to this obnoxious object of his parents' affection slowly. Phrases like, "Let's go diaper *our* baby," are not consistent with what he is thinking. You have brought home a rival, and the less he is forced to cover up his natural competitive feelings the better. The new little baby should be as unheralded as possible while in the presence of your first-born child. He gets nothing from being involved in every diapering, feeding, bathing, or cuddling the baby gets. The new one should not displace him from his bed or disrupt any other routine that he has become comfortable with and accustomed to.

You must remain sensitive to how jealous your first-born child really is. I've worked with many parents who claim that their first-born is "just thrilled" with their new baby. This is usually because of their own wishes to avoid feeling guilty about bringing a competitor into the house. An older child may feign adoration and excessive concern about the welfare of the baby. If so, you are getting off easy for now. But it is extremely likely that the jealousy will show up later. This is totally normal. Jealousy between siblings for parental love and attention is a lifelong reality that is better handled if viewed in its accurate light:

❑ **DON'T REFER TO YOUR ARRIVING** second infant as "Our Baby" or any term that implies that your other child should be as excited for the new arrival as you are. More palatable and neutral terms are "New Sister" or "New Brother."

❑ **NEVER LEAVE A CHILD UNDER** age six or seven alone with your new infant. It is always better to err on the side of cautiousness, even if you think your child isn't angry over having to share his time with you.

❑ **DON'T ASK YOUR OLDEST TO** "help" you attend to and focus your love and attention on the new arrival—if he wants to help you, remind yourself that he is doing this so you will praise him and show how much you love him, not because he adores this "thing" that arrived without his approval.

❑ **OFFER YOUR OLDER CHILD A** new doll to practice diapering, feeding, undressing, powdering, and so on. Once your infant is mobile, help your older child find a baby-proof area to keep his special toys and things away from the crawler.

❑ *NEVER* **COMPARE YOUR KIDS ONE** to another ("Suzy, your brother was able to use the potty by your age"). Don't ever let one child feel that he is being judged in comparison to his brother or sister—*not even favorably*. If you make a favorable comparison like "You are so much more snuggley than your brother," he'll think, "I knew it, I'm better than he is," or, "I feel sorry for my brother." Neither message promotes sibling harmony.

❏ **TRY TO MAKE SURE THAT** each child has his own identity, sphere of friends, special parent adored talents, and individual separate time for parental attention.

When parents strive to treat all their children equally and evenly, they usually fail miserably. First, your children are not the same; they are unique individuals with different ages, interests, problems, and strengths. Promising yourself or your kids that you will treat them all with equality or "fairness" is a ticket to frustration and failure. Don't get yourself into the fairness trap. If you claim that you intend to treat all your kids identically, your kids will watch you like a hawk to be sure they are receiving their fair share—right down to the length of a hug.

Because of different sexes, different personalities, and different birth orders, you are bound to feel differently about each child. It is impossible to love two people equally or in exactly the same way. It's perfectly normal to have different feelings toward different children. If you find yourself secretly preferring one child over another, take another look at your less favored child, seek out what makes him special, and privately share your wonder and appreciation of those qualities with him.

If one of your children complains that you aren't being "fair," respond with something like, "You are absolutely correct. I can never be equal in how I treat you or your sister because each of you is different and what's good for one of you may not be the best thing for the other." What each child needs to hear in this is, "I totally love and adore you because you are special to me and as your 'good boss' I am going to love and discipline you in ways that will help you the best, regardless of how you think I treat the others."

Not Listening, Stubbornness, and Willfulness

If your child appears to not listen, be much more stubborn than other children her age, or seems extremely willful in comparison to her siblings, you will want to get to the root of this difficult behavior. Your first stop should be Appendices #1 and #2 of this book, where you can learn about the interplay between nature and nurture, and the eight categories of temperament. If your child's difficult behaviors are the result of her temperament, you have likely described her from early in her life as being highly active, intense, moody, easily distractible, or very sensitive. If your child's stubbornness is the result of her nature, then you will have to work particularly hard and consistently on Principle #2 to help her gain her goodies—if you don't, then the nature part of her personality will take over in a strong way, and she is likely to have a difficult adulthood.

This behavior could be an indication that your child is showing early signs of ADHD. Please refer to Chapter 8 for a full discussion of this condition. Nonetheless, even if your child appropriately deserves a diagnosis of ADHD, a significant part of the treatment is to apply Principle #2 consistently, firmly, and predictably with as few exceptions or variations as possible.

These cases aside, not listening frequently begins when parents say no to their child or warn him against doing something and then don't follow through when he doesn't pay attention to this. Warning simply doesn't work with children. In addition, try to limit the number of times you say "no" to him. If you say "no" to your child too often, you run the risk of being tuned out. Instead, try to use other words to redirect his attention elsewhere. If you aren't certain whether you should say "no" to something, say something like, "You know, honey, that's a good question. Give

Daddy a minute to think about it. Please don't nag me, because if you do, the answer with be a firm 'no'."

If you do wind up saying "no," say it only once or twice and if he doesn't follow your direction, begin the "goods for goodies" method. Say something like, "I asked you a minute ago to stop that. By continuing, you aren't showing me the goods. Therefore, you will lose TV for the next hour. That will give you time to re-member how to show me respect, ability, good judgment, and self-control." It is important to be consistent in this. Don't take away a goodie one time and then let the same behavior pass the next. Later, when your child shows that he is listening to you, be sure to compliment him on his ability to show you the goods.

Rudeness and Disrespect

A caring parent teaches her child that good manners are essential for good human relations. Sometimes parents make the mistake of not expecting enough respect from their children, making ex-cuses ranging from, "He's just going through a phase" to, "She's so little she can't understand" to, "He's just bored." Two- and three-year-olds are perfectly capable of learning manners and the social graces that help people live well in a society (i.e., politeness, saying "thank you" and "please," etc.), even if they are not able to apply the social graces they learn in one situation to other situa-tions without your assistance. For instance, they may understand that they should say "please" when asking Grandma for some-thing but won't automatically relate that to all situations where they are making a request. When your child approaches five, he is more capable of understanding that politeness makes other people feel better toward you. Five-year-olds are capable of understand-ing other people's viewpoints and feelings. Before this age, they tend to learn manners because it pleases their parents and because by showing these particular goods, they get more goodies. This is an excellent habit, however, to get them into as early as age two.

The key to dealing with rudeness and disrespect is to remember the notion of "goods for goodies." Keep in mind that respect is one of the four foundations of the concept (along with ability, good judgment and self-control). If you consistently show your child what respect means and reinforce it by rewarding it when your child exhibits it, he will also understand why goodies are withheld when he fails to behave in a respectful manner.

For example, every time Carol gets on the phone, her two-year-old Kevin comes up to her demanding juice. Within a few moments, his demands rise in volume to the point where Carol needs to end her conversations early. For a while, Carol excused this behavior as Kevin's being too young to understand better. But she soon began to realize that the consistency of the behavior indicated that Kevin was trying to control his mother, demanding that she pay attention to him rather than the person to whom she was speaking. Two-year-olds are perfectly capable of learning to respect that they must wait to make requests while their parents are speaking to another adult. The next time Kevin made his predictable demand, Carol continued her phone conversation and when she was finished, she said to her son, "Honey, did you show me the goods when you interrupted me on the phone? Did you show me respect by insisting I get you juice when I was talking to Aunt Debby? No, you didn't. Because of that, you will not be able to watch your favorite TV show that starts in a few minutes. Instead, you will help Mommy fold laundry. Maybe next time, you'll remember that when I am on the phone you must wait your turn to talk to me." It took a few tries, but Kevin learned this lesson. A week later, Carol was able to have a complete conversation while Kevin played nearby. When she got off the phone, Carol rewarded this behavior by saying, "Honey, I'm so proud of you for showing me the goods while I was on the phone. Mommy wants to give you an extra special goodie. I want to play your favorite game with you instead of doing what I was planning to do."

"Sassy" and "Mouthy" Behavior

This type of behavior (saying mean or disrespectful things) comes from one of two sources: "thinking errors" that lead to a bad habit of disrespectful behavior or an expression of ambivalence toward one's parents. While the approach to dealing with it is the same, it is useful to understand where it is coming from.

Bad habits often come from "thinking errors" that your child has been allowed to hold. These include:

❑ **HAVING NO CLUE THAT THEIR COMMENTS ARE DISRESPECTFUL.** Children sometimes misunderstand the problems they face and view them without age appropriate insight.

❑ **HAVING DIFFICULTY CONSIDERING ANOTHER PERSON'S POINT OF VIEW.** A child will sometimes magnify the details of a situation that support their point of view while forgetting the other side.

❑ **BLAMING OTHERS FOR WHY THEY ACT A CERTAIN WAY.** These children don't see that their own behaviors are provocative and play a huge role in their own discomfort.

❑ **BELIEVING THEY CAN'T "HELP IT" WHEN THEY HAVE OUTBURSTS.** Children with this thinking error have a habit of not taking responsibility for their own angry or disrespectful behavior.

Ambivalent feelings, on the other hand, come from a child feeling anger toward his parent—a person he loves more than anyone else in the world. From a toddler or preschooler's point of view, it is very normal to feel terribly angry at times and even want to hurt the one he loves the most. In fact, it is this ambivalence, and the fear and guilt stemming from the normal feelings of loving and hating one's parents at the same time, that leads to "back-talk" or "sassy" or "mouthy" comments. Learning to regulate one's ambivalence is an essential step for children. Your child should understand that these feelings are normal while he learns at the same time how to express, direct, and control his intensely conflicted emotions. If he never learns this, he runs the significant risk of turning this anxiety and guilt into unhealthy thoughts and responses. Nothing helps a child more than being able to express hostile and jealous feelings openly, directly, and spontaneously without criticism or condemnation. Teach him that it is okay to express his anger toward you ("I'm mad at you, Mommy"), but that it is *never* okay to use physical violence or disrespectful insults to express his anger. If he does, you need to step in and let him know that he crossed the line.

As noted earlier, whether your child's "sassy" or "mouthy" behavior comes from thinking errors or ambivalent feelings, the way to approach it is the same. The "goods for goodies" method shows your child that no matter how outrageous he acts, you still love him enough to enforce the rules. Sticking firmly to this system and not accepting "sassy" language gives your child the message that you love both him and yourself enough to demand respectful behavior. You are telling your child that he needs to learn better ways to handle emotional stress than lashing out and attacking others. You are teaching him that all people have feelings and that you expect him to learn how to read and respect them in others.

As an example, let's look at five-year-old Tom. Tom heard his parents describe him several times as "having a temper." When Tom became frustrated with something, he let his insulting words fly no matter who got hurt. He figured that was just who he was and his parents' description of him reinforced that. He is making the thinking error of believing he can't help it. His parents can correct this error by saying, "Honey, just now you didn't show us that you could control your own temper. This means you aren't showing us the goods because this doesn't show respect, ability, good judgment, or self-control. Since you didn't show us the goods, you won't be allowed to play on the computer for the rest of the afternoon. We know you are perfectly capable of learning self-control and maybe if you show us later, you'll get more computer time." Later, they'll want to "catch" him showing even a little bit of self-restraint and reward him by saying something like, "Wow, we're impressed with how you're showing us the goods. In the past, you might have gotten really angry when something didn't go your way, but look how you controlled your emotions. For that, you get the goodie of staying up a little later to watch this TV show with us. Good job."

Tattling

Young children are just beginning to develop their conscience and a system of moral values. The blithe comment, "Don't be a tattletale" can therefore be very confusing. Oftentimes when a child reports that someone is doing something wrong, he is looking for justice and confirmation that you also see the act he evaluated as wrong the same way. You can respond with something like, "Yes, it is wrong to take toys away from other people. Thank you for telling me. I'll check into this."

If a child is compulsively reporting on the trivial "wrongdoings" of others, it may be a way of getting attention. Other issues might also be at play. Does he feel so bad about himself that he is seeking to put others down? Is he reporting a forbidden activity as a way of preventing himself from doing it? In these cases, the best response is something like, "Yes, little children often do things they shouldn't do. It takes a long time to learn the rules of life. But that's what grownups can help you with."

When wondering how to handle tattling, think in terms of whether the issue is a little one or a big one. If it's a little issue, clarify the moral doubt or question that may be in the mind of the tattler ("Good for you, honey; you know that a person shouldn't throw her food on the floor"), then let him know that, as a "good boss," you know best how and when to handle it. This makes it clear that you will not use his tattling to allow him to get even, appear more loved, or appear superior in the eyes of his brother or sister or any other child.

If the issue is a big one, thank him for telling you (because you *do* want to hear about the big issues). When you go to deal with the issue, do not tell the offending child how you discovered his indiscretion. Never say something like, "Jimmy, your sister told me that you just wrote on the walls. . . ." Instead, speak directly about the mistake, leaving the tattler's role completely out of it.

Temper Tantrums

Screaming in the middle of a store, throwing things, pulling clothes out of a drawer, making loud demands for things you don't want them to have, and then having a "total fit" when they don't get their way is the kind of behavior in toddlers and preschoolers that can frustrate even the calmest of parents. It is also inevitable. Parents should see tantrums as a way their child releases the excess pent-up energy that emerges as he struggles to become an autonomous human being. Young children use emotional outbursts as a way to discover the boundaries on their behavior. If your child is four and has never had a tantrum, you are probably not teaching him about the realities of life and that normal people have to face situations that frustrate them to the point of rage. The average child aged 18 months to two years has three such outbursts per day. This lessens over time and by age five, boys experience an average of two a day and girls often stop altogether. Tantrums provide parents with a wonderful opportunity to teach a child the necessity of controlling his emotions and that no positive effects come from using this method to try to get your way.

The key to dealing with a temper tantrum is to walk away nonchalantly. It is very difficult for your child to have a successful tantrum without an audience. Once he regains his self-control, you can verbally reward your child for doing so.

The following approaches decidedly *don't* work:

❏ **SPANKING DURING THE TANTRUM.** This teaches the child that in a frustrating situation, the most powerful one wins.

❏ **SCREAMING BACK.** This shows your child that you aren't a "good boss" and are acting just like another child. If you scream at your child when you feel out of control, he will learn this behavior from you.

❏ **OFFERING A CALM EXPLANATION.** Unfortunately doing this while your child is raging is like debating with the ocean waves.

❏ **BRIBERY.** This teaches that tantrums work and sends the message that you will do anything to make one stop.

❏ **LAUGHING OR RIDICULING.** This revs the child up and leaves him feeling scorned and belittled, resulting in his desire to get even later.

❏ **TRYING TO MAKE YOUR CHILD FEEL GUILTY.** Saying something like, "You're hurting Mommy's feelings" does nothing to help him learn self-control and sends the message that he has power over you and you are therefore not a "good boss."

"Time out" is very useful in dealing with tantrums. If the tantrum happens while you are away from home and your usual think-it-over spot, you'll need to improvise. Plan ahead wherever possible. If you think there's a chance your child is going to have a tantrum (most of us know which environments or situations are most likely to trigger this kind of behavior in our children), look around and try to identify a useful "time out" place before anything happens (facing a tree, outside the door of the post office, in the car while you stand calmly outside, in the bathroom, in a vacant hallway).

If public tantrums occur regularly, you can make significant progress by doing even more planning. Try asking your spouse, some other relative, or a caring neighbor to be "on call" for a few hours to drive wherever you are to pick up your child and take him home until you return. Here's an example. Sally was literally afraid to go out in public with three-and-a-half-year-old Tim because he always seemed to have fits at a time that most embarrassed and flustered Sally. This made Sally feel weak and powerless because she knew at some level Tim was totally in charge during these moments. She knew she had to retain her "good boss" status, so she arranged with her sister to be available for a few hours. As they got ready for their outing, she told Tim, "Honey, sometimes you don't show me the goods when we are out. This makes it difficult on Mommy. Today if you aren't able to control yourself and you have a fit, I will call Aunt Suzy and she will take you home. I hope this doesn't happen because at the end of the shopping trip, if you show me the goods, we'll go for ice cream as a goodie." Just as Sally guessed, when she went to a counter to buy something, Tim began making demands and having a fit. Sally said, "Honey, if you don't show me the goods by the time I count to ten, I will have to call Aunt Suzy." Tim's fit continued, probably because he figured he was in charge. Sally left the checkout line, calmly took out her cell phone and, in front of Tim, asked her sister to come pick Tim up. Within a few minutes, Tim calmed down and promised to be good. Sally knew, though, that one calm gentle lesson like this would be priceless. She said, "Honey, I'm sorry that you weren't able to show me the goods by controlling your fit soon enough. I'm sorry I can't give you the goodie of ice cream. But Aunt Suzy will take you home and I'll be there soon." Tim learned an invaluable lesson that day.

He learned he had a really good boss.

The problem behaviors covered in this chapter can feel overwhelming to parents, driving a parent to question his ability to function. Parents must respond consistently and predictably to these behaviors, as would any good boss or teacher. Good bosses are in control—they never let their staff believe they are overwhelmed or clueless as to how to handle a situation. Good bosses demand respect while demonstrating full regard for those under them.

Proper discipline is essential for a child's developing personality. Through appropriate discipline, a child learns self-control, self-direction, and a sense of caring. Structures, limits and routines help kids develop a sense of predictability, capacity for self-regulation, and restraint. Children feel safe when they feel safely contained within your rules and structures.

There is no such thing as an inverse relationship between Principle #1 and Principle #2. It is not true that the more one loves the less one can or should discipline or that the more one disciplines the less one can love. In fact, the more one disciplines in a consistent way following Principle #2, the more you are showing your love toward your child—because disciplining properly takes almost Herculean consistency, patience, and effort.

CHAPTER 6

Parenting Principle #3: Prepare Them for the Real World

No matter how much you might want to protect your child forever in the protective cocoon of home, at some point, he is going to have to encounter the real world. Therefore, while it might not be desirable, it is essential that you prepare your child for what is required of him by society. For many parents Principle #3 is the toughest Principle to follow. Using Principle #3 we must teach our children that we will give them what they need, not necessarily what they want, that it is not our role to make sure they are always happy, that they must learn to experience and handle the frustrations of life, that they must learn to cope with the unfairness of life, that we accept and support their growing independence, that we want them to understand the importance of being part of a larger community, and that their parents have relationships separate from them. None of these things is easy for a loving parent to do, but all of them are vital. Introducing your child to the real world while still under your protection is far better than hiding him from harsh realities and then releasing him into the world to learn lessons from strangers who will not be so kind and loving in their method of teaching.

An important note: to teach your toddler or preschooler properly about the real world, you must remind yourself about the way she thinks. Toddlers remain focused primarily on their present reality and have only a vague concept of past, present, or future. They tend to view things as either painful or pleasurable and they tend to view their own abilities as either they can or can't. A preschooler's thinking is rigid. She views ideas, rules, and concepts as either black or white with little to no gray areas.

Additionally, toddlers and preschoolers have a lot of trouble seeing the world from another person's point of view. Until about the age of six or seven, children have a limited (though developing) ability to think abstractly. For example, imagine a typical preschooler seated at a table opposite another person. Imagine that upon this table sits two different toys separated by an opaque piece of cardboard. A toy car is visible only to the seated child and a doll is visible only to the other person. If you ask the preschooler to walk around the table and see what the other person sees and then have him return to his seat facing the toy car, and then ask him what toy the other person can see, frequently the preschooler will say, "The car." This is because he has not yet completely developed his ability to view things from another person's perspective. Our job as parents of toddlers and preschoolers then is to help them view the world as realistically as possible within the realities of how much they are able to grasp.

Give Your Child What He Needs, Not What He Wants

Having the "gimmes" is reaching epidemic proportions in our country and parents are both contributing to this disease and falling victim to its symptoms. Parents often incorrectly believe that if they don't give their children everything they want, they are depriving them. Loving authority figures want their children to be happy. It is essential, however, to think of your child's *wants* as entirely different from her *needs*. She *needs* the things covered by Principles #1 and #2—touch, eye contact, dedicated time, and appropriate discipline. Give her as much of this as you can. Wants are another issue entirely. Give her something when you believe she has shown you the goods and you think it is appropriate to grant a goodie. This does not mean, though, that you are obligated to grant every one of her wants when she behaves well. In fact, if you do this, your child's personality will suffer.

Parents sometimes believe that they owe their child whatever they want. This is wrong. To be a good parent, we actually "owe" our children what I like to call BASIC parenting:

- ❑ B (basic nutritional foods adequate for good growth).

- ❑ A (absence of emotional, physical, and sexual abuse).

- ❑ S (safety and secure base love—Principle #1).

- ❑ I (instruction in schooling and home discipline—Principle #2).

- ❑ C (clothing for protection).

That is *all*. Anyone providing BASIC parenting to his or her child can look herself in the mirror each morning and know she is being a good parent.

Everything beyond BASIC parenting is a goodie. Do you see designer clothing on this list? Do you see popular fast food meals or expensive specialty food on this list? Do you see select pricey private preschool attendance here? Do you see sweets, countless toys, endless parties, continual organized sports activities, innumerable lessons, etc.? No. They are things our children might want and which we might love to give them. However, since giving them things is so much easier and more pleasurable to our souls than teaching them about consequences, reality, self-denial, self-restraint, and self-discipline, we must be very cautious that we are not giving them more than what is good for them.

Overindulged children have been given too much or have been given into too often. Giving your child extra time as a goodie (an entire day at the pool, playing with them for an extended period in the backyard, time with them at the movies, playing their favorite board game, etc.) when they have shown you the goods rarely leads to overindulgence. However, giving them too many material things (particularly when you have set the bar for showing the goods too low) can be terribly destructive to their personalities.

Overindulged (a.k.a., spoiled) children are extremely vulnerable to emotional problems. A spoiled child is an anxious child searching for limits and relief from his own demands. Spoiled children:

❏ Are difficult to be around because they tend to be self-centered and unaware of others' feelings.

❏ Use the powerful words, "I'm bored" often because they received so much in their childhood they lack creativity and resourcefulness.

❏ Lack an accurate perception of how they are coming across to others.

❏ Rarely take responsibility for their actions.

❏ Believe that the value of human relationships is dependent upon money and things.

❏ Have trouble making and sustaining true relationships with others—they tend to relate to others in a very superficial way.

❑ Get "used" by others a lot because they are so unaware of themselves and others.

❑ Rarely follow through on a project to its successful completion—they become addicted to the constant stimulation of newness so that when a project requires time-consuming work they usually want to move on.

❑ Are terribly insecure about themselves and their own worth and tend to have a deep need for acceptance and approval by others.

❑ Tend not to learn how to take care of things and property responsibly because they have gotten used to just getting a replacement or something better when something breaks or needs upkeep; they often apply this cavalier attitude to others' property.

❑ Tend to be very deceitful since they are rarely held accountable for their actions; as they get older they tend to use half-truths, omission, obscure excuses, passive manipulation, and outright lies to get away with things.

❑ Often eschew the future as not worth worrying about.

❑ Are frequently very angry as older children and adults when the real world doesn't continue to give them whatever they want.

Sometimes parents buy their children whatever others have. This is a terrible curse, because it teaches conformity rather than the development of more important character traits (such as self-restraint, self-control, humility, generosity, empathy, self-assurance, etc.). After all, your child will encounter those with "more" her entire life. If you raise your child to believe she always deserves the best immediately and/or she always deserves whatever others have, she is doomed to be continually disappointed and/or have less regard for the blessings she already has.

If you find your child demanding whatever others have you might say something like, "Honey, I see that Johnny always seems to have the latest and greatest toys. But he is missing something big that you have. Mommy and Daddy love you so much we are willing to help you learn about the real world. All your life others will have more of one thing or another than you do. That doesn't mean they will be happier than you will. Look at all the wonderful toys and people you have in your life. Oftentimes people who get whatever they want are unhappy because they do not appreciate what they have." I once said something like this to one of my kids who responded, "Mommy, could you love me a little less and give me what I want?" I laughed and hugged her, and though she was unhappy with me for a while, I was confident that she would grow up to appreciate that she was getting what she needed from me.

Just a short word about spoiling and the role of grandparents: *while it is the role of the parents to never spoil their child, it is the grandparents' main role to* always *spoil the child.* If your child's grandparents elect to load her up with toys and she comes home "wild" from the freedoms she encounters with them, you should not rage against this—especially within your child's earshot. Instead, use this as an opportunity to discuss the real world with your child. Say something like, "Honey, your grandma and grandpa love you and you all have a great time together. When you are at their house, you get to have a vacation from the rules and responsibilities of life. But when you get home, your vacation is over and you have to adjust to the rules here at home. Do you need to spend time in your room to have a chance to chill out?"

Do Not Try to Keep Your Child "Happy"

Some of the unhappiest children I have ever worked with come from families where the parents have told me they believed it was their role to keep their kids happy. Too often, when we try to keep a child happy we do this because we can't stand to see them unhappy. This is unwise. Children need to understand that the real world will cause them to be unhappy many times and that they need to learn to express their genuine emotions about their pain rather than covering it up or avoiding it.

The child whose parents have catered to his demands expressed through crying or temper is likely to believe that his place in the world is assured as long as people are serving him. Kids who have been "kept happy" by their parents become more and more sullen and demanding every year. Pampered kids fail to learn self-discipline because they don't get the opportunities to make their own mistakes and learn from the consequences. Kids whose parents fear their unhappiness often end up angry with their parents when they realize they haven't adequately learned to run their own lives or make their own decisions. Remember, true happiness comes from doing great things that make us proud of ourselves, not receiving great things from others.

Often, when we apply Principle #2 and remove a freedom or favor, our kids become very angry with us. The experience of getting angry with us at times is actually healthy for them. Stick with your decision. Do not crumple because you are afraid of their displeasure. It is healthy for children to experience their sad, mad, or bad emotions with the ones they love. This will teach them the inevitable reality that all humans at times both love and hate those closest to them. Stand firm and teach them that you love them anyway. Remind yourself that you love your child so much you are willing to allow him to be very angry or unhappy on his journey to learning how to become a responsible person.

Allow Your Kids to Experience and Handle Frustration

The real world contains tons of frustrations that every adult, even hugely successful adults, must deal with every day. Healthy adults have learned how to tolerate frustration and persevere in spite of it. This is a necessary quality for adults that children must learn when they are young.

How do we introduce our kids to a frustration that is good for them? Well, to begin with, many parents today give their children much more than they can ever expect to get as adults. Adults rarely achieve or receive even half of the items they wish for (the house of their dreams, the super-expensive car, the ideal job, the perfect spouse, unending vacations, wildly successful sex, the flawless body, etc.). Yet many parents believe they should give their children everything they wish. Oftentimes when a child wants a toy or gadget, the parents believe they are letting their child down if they don't give it to him promptly. As a result, the child grows up thinking if she wants something, she should get it. This pattern of thinking is a recipe for an unhappy frustrated adult.

Getting too much for too little teaches a child values that will handicap her in the real world. To succeed as an adult, our toddlers and preschoolers must understand that if they want something badly enough, they must be willing to work hard for it. Parents must insist that their children see their obligations (their chores, their committed interests) through to the end. For example, imagine that your preschooler has begged you for a pet and you are amenable to this idea. You should discuss fully before obtaining the pet what you view her role to be in the pet's maintenance (while keeping in mind realistic age appropriate expectations). If she commits to fulfilling a certain role toward the pet's maintenance, you must hold her accountable. If she doesn't meet her obligation, you must employ the goods-for-goodies method. To let her off the hook is to give her false expectations about the real world. It is essential for parents to teach that there is a link between effort and reward. If the lesson frustrates your child, remember that she is also learning important things.

Experiencing frustration and learning how to handle it allows the child to learn that meaningful feelings of happiness can come from within themselves, not from external material items. True happiness comes from a secure and confident belief in our own ability to affect others in a positive way. True happiness does not come from how many things we have. The more external things a child gets, particularly when the child gets them with very little of his own effort, the more misdirected the child becomes in learning about what truly brings happiness and contentment to a person. Show me a child who gets many things for very little of his own effort, and I'll show you an unhappy child who doesn't take good care of those things. Why should he? He has gotten used to a world where things just keep coming to him regardless of how little energy he expends.

Conflict is the normal state of affairs for adults (should I major in this or that; shall I move here or there; shall I marry or focus on my career; should we have one child or more, etc.). Every day of our adult lives, we must choose one course of action while forgoing other attractive choices. Asking your child to choose between two competing activities, both of which she desires, allows her to learn that a normal human often "cannot have their cake and eat it too." For example, you are doing an excellent job of teaching her Principle #3 when you say something like, "Honey, today we have time to let your friend come over and play or Daddy can take you to the zoo." When the inevitable begging begins about wanting to do both, you can explain the normal frustrations inherent in life in ways she can understand. For example, you might say, "I understand how disappointing it is when you have to choose between two things you really want. But in life we have to make lots of choices—we can't do all the fun things there are to do." Kids need to experience making a choice and adjusting to the disappointment of not having the other choice. Learning they cannot have all they want makes them more prepared for the realities of the real world.

Parents show an enormous love for their child when they allow him to make a mistake and experience real life consequences. Oftentimes the most loving thing you can do is to stand quietly by and let your toddler or preschooler discover natural consequences on his own. Kids allowed to make their own mistakes (that subsequently cause them some level of unhappiness) are kids who will wind up making far fewer mistakes as they grow older. For example, your child wants to tie a balloon to his own wrist and won't tolerate your help. You stand by patiently as he valiantly and perhaps stubbornly tries to tie the string. When his treasured balloon flies off into the atmosphere, he learns about real world consequences. When this happens, offer him comfort and an accurate description of what happened and how he is feeling ("Yes, honey, I tried to help you tie that but you wanted to do it by yourself. Balloons not properly tied often blow away. You wanted that balloon and it's sad that you don't have it now."). Do not buy him another balloon. He needs to experience the emotions that result from his actions.

Learning to Cope with the Unfairness of Life

In *The Road Less Traveled*, Dr. M. Scott Peck says, "Life is difficult. This is a great truth, one of the greatest truths. . . . Life is a series of problems. Do we want to moan about them or solve them? Do we want to teach our children to solve them? What makes life difficult is that the process of confronting and solving problems is a painful one."

Dr. Peck advises that we must teach our children how to deal directly with life's problems using four tools:

- ❏ Delaying gratification (developing and applying self-discipline).

- ❏ Accepting responsibility for one's own actions and problems (not blaming others).

- ❏ Dedication to truth and reality (continual self-evaluation and self-correction).

- ❏ Balancing (flexibly dealing with conflicting needs, goals, and responsibilities).

Some children encounter unfortunate experiences early in their lives. However, parents must never pity or feel sorry for their children. When you feel sorry for your child, no matter how justifiable this reaction may be, you teach your child that she has a right to feel sorry for herself—a feeling that will bring her much misery. A child who is allowed to feel sorry for herself is a child who has been led to believe that life owes her something and that she has a right to demand more and more. This demanding attitude greatly undermines her ability to function in the world. Instead, give empathy when your child has just learned an important life lesson. Consequences and empathy together maximizes the child's ability to learn about the real world.

Handle Your Kids the Way the World Will

Well-meaning parents who give their child virtually whatever he wants are not raising a child with the values and skills necessary for a successful fulfilled life. Such children often suffer tremendously from culture shock when they leave their parents' artificial home environment (where they are required to contribute and achieve very little) and enter a real world that demands a tolerance for frustration and perseverance that overindulged children lack.

Being "real" means you teach your child that he is not the center of the universe. If you have a child who demands too much, ask yourself, "Is he this way because I am afraid to have him not love me?" Parents must not expect that their children will like them every minute of every day. Parents who need approval, acceptance, or adoration from their children all the time are in for real trouble. These parents are often afraid to deny their child's requests for fear of angering or hearing the dreaded words, "Then I won't love you." Love begotten through bribery or blackmail is not genuine. Parents should never beg for their child's love, or try to placate their child by being overly permissive "just so he won't be mad at me." If you think this might apply to you, read Chapter 10 about healing your own wounds.

Remember that there are two types of love: fundamental love and affectionate love. Remind your child that your fundamental love for her is forever, solid, unwavering, and unconditional. At the same time, though, remind her that your other type of love, your affectionate love for her, *is* conditional. To give a child the message that you love her affectionately without her having to meet any obligations of returning your love is to raise a child who will be self-centered to the point of being miserable to be around. Self-centered children grow up to be adults with serious relationship problems. After all, who wants to be with a spouse who is so in love with herself that she is unwilling to alter her behavior to make herself more lovable?

Toddlers and preschoolers must learn that there are obligations in love; that love is given but also earned. Teach your child that sometimes he has a chance to undo a mistake and solve a problem by making amends. In some situations when your toddler or preschooler has erred and not shown you the goods, you may want to allow him to earn a special goodie he can receive after he has finished living out his consequence. If you choose this path, let him help you problem solve on how he can earn a special freedom or favor from you. For example, you might say to your child, "Honey, when you didn't show me the goods by having a tantrum, it drained a lot of energy out of me, even though you lost your goodies. What ideas do you have to fill my energy level back up? If you can figure out how to fill Mommy's energy level, then maybe Mommy will feel good enough to let your friend have a play date with you this afternoon." This is real world stuff. Adults are sometimes able to "fix" problems in their lives (pay fines, apologize, repair broken things, etc.), so it is good practice to allow your child the opportunity and experience of fixing their mistakes to your satisfaction.

This feels good to your child because she feels a sense of pride and self-respect that she is able to fix her problem. A caution here: do not let her earn back the goodies you took away as a consequence or she will figure that the removal of her goodies is always a temporary state of affairs that can be undone by being good, begging, or acting unhappy. Help your child understand that after she experiences her loss of goodies that you told her would happen, that she may be allowed to earn a special treat afterwards only in those special circumstances when she has expended a lot of extra effort. Do not give her a special treat every time she loses a goodie or she will think she has you "all figured out" and become manipulative.

Accept Your Child's Emerging Independence

Perhaps the hardest realization in all of parenting is the bittersweet acknowledgment that if we do our job correctly, our children will have the strength and confidence to leave us to live their own lives and make their own decisions. This realization requires a very difficult journey for many parents. At the beginning of their lives, their children have an intense and complete physical closeness and dependency upon them. For many parents, this feels overwhelmingly good. Some parents feel happier than they have ever felt. There is a basic joy and satisfaction in having another human completely dependent upon you and this good feeling often interferes with our rational ability to do what we know we must do: raise our children to be able to separate from us in a healthy way.

While your child comes from both of his parents, he is also developing into his own being with his own dreams, aspirations, and goals that are likely different from yours. You must be willing to *feel separate* from your child in order to be able to help him in the best way possible. If your own life is full and you are secure in your identity, it is much easier to hold the following truth close to your heart: *I have my own life that is separate from my child's and right now I am sharing my life with my child.*

There's a metaphor I use to help people envision their parenting role and the amount of connection they have with their child. When your child is born, she begins life still connected to her mother through an umbilical cord. For the next few months, you have ultimate control over her every activity and she has no freedoms in her life. The umbilical cord connection between you is still short. In her toddler and preschooler years, the umbilical cord begins to lengthen. During her childhood, the umbilical cord gets even longer. Throughout her childhood years, you as the parent adjust the cord length—you tighten it when she needs to be closer to you or when she doesn't show you the goods and you need to constrain her freedom and you loosen it when her behaviors demonstrate respect, ability, good judgment, and self-control. As she grows older and matures, you lengthen the cord significantly to include more and more freedoms and more of the real world. As she enters adulthood, you symbolically cut the umbilical cord.

You must keep in mind your end goal—that your child will leave your home and you will cut his cord completely. Your healthy child will become a separate individual from you—no more umbilical connection to you ever. This doesn't mean that he will not be tightly connected to you. What this does mean is that the healthy adult-child's final decisions and self-control come from within himself (even if he continues to ask his parents for wisdom and input), not from his parents' ability to control him.

Parents who try to retain too much control as a child grows up raise a child who mightily and painfully rebels, often with disastrous consequences. Parents who "lengthen the cord" too fast raise a child who flounders and makes painful (often lingering or permanent) mistakes because she lacks the skills to handle so much freedom. Because your child is growing and evolving into her own separate being, you must be willing to watch and see what develops. Instead of wanting your child to become something in particular, just want her to *become*. Think of your role as a parent as that of a good farmer who reaches into a barrel of hundreds of types of seeds and plants one seed not knowing exactly what will develop. While this farmer does not know what type of seed he has chosen from the barrel, he knows that his seed needs soil, water, and sun to varying degrees. The wise farmer tends closely to his budding seed, adapting his gardening techniques to the characteristics that seem to help his little seed best. The wise farmer watches closely to see what emerges from the ground and adjusts his farming skills accordingly. More or less sun? More or less water? Sandy or rich soil? Following Principle #3, your "farming" technique should be one that accepts your child as a separate individual who should be prepared in the best way possible to face the real world.

Communicate to Promote Your Child's Emerging "Being"

How we talk to our children can make a huge difference in how our child perceives and learns to function in the real world. In many ways, almost everything we say to our children is a "teaching conversation." It is through these conversations that they learn how to appraise their thoughts, feelings, actions, and plans.

Many parents are unaware of how they really talk to their children. If you need a reality check, put a tape recorder in the room with you and your child and listen to it later alone or with your spouse. You may be amazed to hear someone who sounds like a drill sergeant using your voice: "Don't do that . . . sit up straight . . . stop that . . . no . . . cut it out! . . . be quiet . . . not now . . . I mean it! . . . stop acting like that . . . I'm warning you . . . do it this way . . . come on . . . here, like this. . . ." Kudos to those parents who have the guts to listen to themselves talk. It takes a great deal of courage to be willing to look at how many times we fail to communicate acceptance to our children. Children who feel unaccepted by us become insecure and under-prepared to face the real world.

Four main communication techniques have a huge impact on how prepared your child is to meet the real world:

❏ **HANDLING INTENSE EMOTIONS WITH "THE MIRACLE RESPONSE."** Strong emotions are like rivers: you can divert them, but not stop them. You cannot ignore or reason away your child's intense feelings; you must acknowledge them. Try talking to your child using what I call "The Miracle Response": reflecting back your child's strong emotions when he is in the midst of them. When a child is in the midst of feelings of this sort, he is not open to advice or criticism. Accept his unique feelings by acknowledging, identifying, recognizing, and/or repeating those feelings back to him. Convey to your child that you recognize his feeling and (if even for only a moment) feel his pain. This is empathy.

For example, imagine your child just burned himself on the stove after you warned him not to touch it. What your child really needs when he is hurting is to have someone acknowledge his inner pain and give him a chance to talk about it. Accept the way your child is feeling instead of trying to get rid of the feeling. If you say, "Ooh, that must really hurt. I can see how much that hurts you," you are merely observing or reflecting back his own feelings in a way that shows you feel some of his pain. This is what empathy is all about.

On the other hand, many responses are not empathetic. For example, if you were to say, "Oh it's not so bad. It's not even red," your trying to reassure him or minimize his pain makes him feel like you don't understand him. If you say, "Oh, stop crying and being such a baby," you have ridiculed or attempted to minimize his pain by trying to deny his own feelings that are very real to him. If you say, "Shhhh. Everybody is looking; now hush!" you are trying to distract him or make him feel guilty or wrong for having his own real feelings. If you say, "Yes, life is like that. You will have many burns in your life," you give him philosophy when he is least able to hear you and he will feel that you aren't hearing his pain. If you say, "Oh, you poor thing. I feel so sorry for you," you have made him feel pitiful.

Your child must be allowed to feel OK about having and expressing his feelings no matter what he is feeling. Allow your child to express these in the comfort of your presence. Remember, words and feelings are not the same as actions . . . allow your child to express his emotions without fearing them. Acknowledged feelings go away sooner and better than feelings that are denied, criticized, or stifled. The most loving thing a parent can do for a child is to allow the child to experience his feelings fully even if this causes you discomfort and pain.

Empathy is not about trying to fix his emotions. Instead, it's about letting him know you have really *heard* his emotions. When your child believes that you have truly heard his feeling, he will feel understood and will be much more prepared to go out into the real world. Children who feel misunderstood often act out their frustrations on others as they grow up. Empathizing helps a child accept a situation he cannot change.

❑ **FRAMING WHAT IS HAPPENING TO HER TO MAXIMIZE HER LEARNING.** Properly "framing" life lessons is critical to your child's learning about the world. For example, suppose you spent time throwing the ball with your three-year-old. She will undoubtedly really enjoy her time with you. You will receive more "bang for the buck," however, and build a higher sense of self-worth in your little one if you verbally frame your actions for her. For example, if during and after playing with her you say: "Honey, I really enjoy spending time with you. Right now you are really fun to be with," you feed the growth of her self-esteem and help her understand that when she acts well socially, others enjoy spending time with her. Interpreting this activity for your child makes the experience much more positive for her and helps her see how the real world views her. If you fail to frame her experiences with you and others, she will probably miss many opportunities to understand her and others' actions and feelings. For example, without the above framing he might make a thinking error such as, "My mommy is throwing the ball with me because I cried hard a few minutes ago."

Framing your responses so your child can understand another person's way of viewing things is invaluable. Children who don't often receive a framing of what just happened and why often take longer to learn the lessons of life. Help your child be "lifewise."

❏ **DESCRIBING INSTEAD OF JUDGING HIS ACTIVITIES AND INTERESTS.** Parents often intrude too much on their kids' interests and activities. When parents intrude by interfering, directing, advising, warning, lecturing, suggesting, preaching, judging, criticizing, commanding, or giving solutions, they fail to communicate an acceptance of their child. Allow your child to discover his world of interests and activities by himself as much as possible. Kids who believe they are accepted for their "being" are those who are allowed to explore their own interests and activities without parental judgments.

For example, imagine that your toddler or preschooler has just discovered a puzzle. The accepting parent is the one who stands back and lets the child explore the puzzle in his own way by merely describing what he sees ("Oh, what an interesting puzzle you have there."). The accepting parental response of *describing, not judging* allows the child to explore new activities in his own separate and independent way. He may choose to become very involved in the puzzle, or he may choose to ignore it and move to another activity. Either way, an accepting response from his parent allows the child to become his own being by expressing interest in what he enjoys instead of selecting activities or interests that please his parents more than him. Suppose your child is looking at this puzzle and you as a parent have always wanted your child to love and be good at puzzles. Be very careful here—whose goal is it? Kids asked to conform to their parents' activities or interests are kids who will oftentimes later expend tremendous energy in rebelling.

Compare the accepting response of describing, not judging to the following "non-accepting" responses:

➤ "Here, let me help you put it together" (ordering, directing, commanding, imposing).

➤ "Here is what it should look like. Shouldn't you put that piece in next?" (advising, lecturing, preaching, offering solutions, analyzing, diagnosing).

➤ "Don't you want to spend more time with this?" or "Aren't you ready to do something else?" (judging, moralizing, disagreeing, interfering, questioning, probing, diverting).

➤ "You are capable of putting together more pieces than this" (criticizing, threatening, admonishing, warning, arguing, blaming, shaming, ridiculing).

Try to decrease your judgment comments on your child's activities and instead stick with accepting comments. Your child will likely blossom into doing those things that really interest him rather than spending time stressing about whether or not his interests will please or displease his parents.

❏ **PRAISING HIS BEING, NOT HIS DOING.** The majority of the praise your tot or preschooler receives should be verbal praise totally unrelated to her achievement or success. Isn't this the type of praise that we as adults most value? After all, which praise feels more special and important to you: when your spouse praises a meal you spent a couple of hours preparing, or when you walk into the room and she greets you with an unexpected, "I've been just thinking how happy I am to be with you!" While both types of praise feel good, the latter is more deeply meaningful because it is directed more at your real "being" and less at your actions. If you hear praise for the meal you just cooked, you may think to yourself, "Gosh, I wonder if she expects this type of meal every day? I wonder if she is so amazed at this meal because she has disliked the ones before this? What if I can't live up to her new expectations and am only able to cook her a mediocre meal tomorrow?"

If you feel "loved" because of an accomplishment, you live in terror that you will lose this skill, beauty, fame, or honor. If you feel "loved" because you exist, you feel wonderful. *Instead of praising your child's accomplishments, try simply noticing them.* Kids respond better if the majority of the time you don't judge what they are doing. For example, imagine that preschooler Jane is drawing a picture and you want to give her a compliment. What you say makes a difference in what she likely thinks to herself. If you say, "I notice you like to draw that pretty flower. Wow, you sure look like you enjoy drawing," Jane may think to herself, "I am valued because Daddy noticed me and what I am doing."

Incorrect praise can actually stop the interest in something because of the child's fear that she might disappoint you. For example, if you say, "You are such a great artist!" Jane is likely to think to herself, "Uh oh, maybe he'll think that the next picture I draw isn't so good. I'm kind of scared to draw another one because he might not like it as much!" Praising everything Jane draws does not work either; the praise will become meaningless to her. The other possibility is that Jane will form such a false impression of her drawing ability that she will likely have trouble hearing any realistic critique or constructive comments from others.

Praise has the potential to fill a toddler or preschooler's soul with pleasure and pride. Praise done correctly confirms for your child his inherent value as a human on this earth.

Teach about the Joy in Being Part of a Larger Community

How you introduce your toddler or preschooler to the world is important. Children who are taught that there is trouble lurking around every corner or that that anyone who is not just like them is "evil" or a "lesser human" are being handicapped in terrible ways. Think about the messages you pass on to your children. The majority of Americans are kind, generous, interesting folks of all sizes, ages, colors, and ethnicities. Yet if you watch the news with your child and stress over the terrible state of the world without counterbalancing this with a message of love and tolerance toward others, you give your child a strong message that the world is a fearful place. This is a horrendous burden to place upon his shoulders.

I am not suggesting that you forgo the logical lessons of wise parents (don't go somewhere with strangers without our blessing, don't walk alone at night, don't invite strangers at the door into our home, etc.). However, to give your child the message that anyone could be a kidnapper or every person who says "hi" to them on the street probably has evil intentions is to raise a child who never feels safe. Good parents model for their child friendly interaction with strangers. Seeing this, they learn that they are part of a larger community that needs their participation and nurturance. They need to learn (through watching their parents) that they should respect the rights and dignity of others. When children experience and participate in their community, they feel safer and more secure in the world.

Successful families teach their children at a very early age that generosity and doing good deeds is an important part of life. You should help your child discover the value of themselves through helping others. Have her help you bake cookies for a neighbor who just had a family tragedy. Have her help you collect used items to donate "to those who have less than we do." Teach your child that by helping others, a person develops a good feeling about herself. Children never exposed to the value of helping others are doomed to become arrogant and this behavior often leads to a lifetime of unhappiness. Arrogant children often have a terrible time making and sustaining friends because they turn people off with their attitudes.

Your young child should discover that contributing to the welfare of others has many personal rewards. For one thing, helping others is a critical aspect of a person's self-esteem. Serving the needs of your infant and young child makes you feel better about yourself as a parent. Your child has similar feelings. Teach your child that by "helping" Mommy or Daddy in a million ways every day (hugging, cooperating, loving, etc.) he makes you feel better. This will help him feel better about himself. This reciprocal relationship of giving and getting, receiving and loving back is what builds the positive relationship between parents and their children and people and their communities. This giving and receiving is an important key to one's self-esteem and the reason that helping others feels so good. Teach your child by modeling giving behavior (to your church, synagogue, community center, neighbors, etc.). Teach your child how good a person feels when you experience helping and then receiving positive feedback from others.

Nurture and Maintain a Healthy Relationship between the Parents

Parents are the center of the universe for their young children. For you, though, the marriage relationship between mom and dad should be center stage, not the "wants" of the kids. A healthy respectful relationship between mother and father is essential for the well-being and mental health of children. When parents forget to take care of themselves and their relationship, they put their kids at risk.

From their early toddler years, children need to learn that their parents have a private life together that does not include them. If both parents are together in the family, the bond and relationship between these two parents is the model through which your children will view the world. If the bond is sacred and respectful the majority of the time, the kids will feel safe and good about themselves. Conversely, if there is a great deal of tension and disrespect in the home or between two separated parents, the kids will feel unsafe, will learn to dislike themselves, and will likely act out their stress through difficult behaviors. (A healthy relationship between the two parents is also critical even if they are no longer together. I will cover how to parent in divorce situations in Chapters 9 and 10).

Work on your marital relationship in whatever way you know will enhance it. Marriages frequently suffer when small children are in the house because one or both of the spouses forget to prioritize the marriage. Be sure your communication and your sexual relationship is meeting the needs of *both* parents. Both parents should respect the intimacy and adult communication needs of the other and be willing to answer the other partner's need even if it isn't the top priority in their mind. Get help from others if necessary to allow you both to recapture the enthusiasm for the relationship you probably once had.

A healthy and respectful marital relationship takes time. Prioritize the time to share in intimacy and communication. This doesn't mean an extended vacation away from your kids. It does mean, however, that you may need a night a week or a weekend away to rekindle the bond between you. Your child will likely initially resent it when you leave him for a night out, but you should help him understand that his parents have a life separate from him.

You can say something like this: "Honey, both Mommy and Daddy love you. We both love each other, too. To help us be the best parents we can be for you, we need to spend special time together. You will be safe with _____ and we'll come kiss you when we get home tonight."

This approach is almost certain to meet with some resistance from your child. She wants to be the sole center of your universe. But you are meeting one of her needs as part of Principle #3. Your child must not think she runs the family or that her wishes are her parents' commands. If both of her parents are together, she must understand that the relationship between the parents is a sacred relationship in the family so that each parent can give her what she needs. It is healthy for your child to know that you love her and cherish her, have a lifelong commitment to her, and will always give her what she needs, but that she is not the only person at the center of your life. Helping your child understand this is an incalculably valuable gift because this helps her to grow, evolve and become her own person in charge of her own life.

As we have all learned in our lives, the real world is a difficult place filled with challenges and obstacles. So too is teaching our children about the real world. Unfortunately, if you don't teach your child the realities of life while he is still under your protection, he will emerge from your nest either considering himself to be the "center of the universe" or viewing the world as a nice place obligated to satisfy his every wish. Such self-centeredness leads quickly to feelings of anger, rebellion, and depression. Introducing your children to the realities of the world is an important task that is oftentimes incredibly difficult for parents because it requires one's own restraint, self-sacrifice and delayed gratification in order to provide a greater lesson. Take comfort in knowing that these lessons—when combined with Principles #1 and #2—will give your child a rock solid foundation upon which to base his life as an individual.

CHAPTER 7

Putting Principle #3 to Work

In this chapter, you will find ten problem behaviors that are most helped by paying special attention to Principle #3. My recommendations here essentially fall into two categories. The first relates to your calming down, having patience, and showing faith that your child will follow his innate capacity for growing and changing. The second advises a decrease in permissiveness and need to please your child. This second category might require you to do a considerable amount of personal work. If you discover that you are parenting in a weak or overly permissive way, you will likely face quite a challenge in adjusting. Still, it is critical. Children who are spoiled, controlling, or irresponsible enter high school with emotional problems that play out in serious ways.

The behaviors discussed in this chapter are:

❑ Controlling behavior and being bossy

❑ Demanding, acting spoiled, or begging

❑ Endless fantasy and imaginary friends

❑ Lying and stealing

❑ Not talking and shyness

❑ Picky eating or refusing to eat

❑ Sexual curiosity and masturbation

❑ Struggling about chores

❑ Toilet training woes and bedwetting

❑ Whining and nagging

Controlling Behavior and Being Bossy

Controlling or bossy kids become this way for a reason. There are several potential reasons why:

❑ Parents fear anger or sadness in their child and therefore give in to all of his demands.

❑ Parents feel guilty about the lack of time they have to spend with their child or the lack of interest they have in spending quality time with their child.

❑ The child does it to fill a parenting void. This often happens in divorce situations where one parent or the other tries to "win" the child by being overly permissive.

❑ The child does not feel safe or secure in his household. If her home is too stressful, she will attempt to control things out of fear that doing anything less could cause her harm.

Regardless of the cause, the cure for all controlling or bossy children is to garner the strength to fulfill your parenting duties properly—including enduring your child's disapproval, anger, rage, or sadness. If this seems insurmountable, read Chapter 10 on healing your own wounds. If you are divorced and disagree with your former spouse on how to handle your child, refer to Chapter 9. You may need to seek additional professional help to overcome your child's power.

Your controlling child will put you to the test to see who is really in control. Hold firm and remember that the earlier you start this process the better for both of you. You will most likely need to resort to BASIC parenting for a while. Give your child what she needs while severely limiting her goodies. Tell her what is going on in an age appropriate way so she understands what is happening to her. When she shows that she is adjusting to this "new attitude," you can offer her more freedom and favors. If the controlling behavior returns, however, go right back to BASIC.

This technique *really works*. Countless parents I have worked with who have used this approach have found a dramatic improvement in their child's behavior. It's tough and may require a ton of parenting effort for a while, but you have few other acceptable options. Always remember that you are sparing your child an unhappy adulthood where people shun her for her unbearably entitled attitude toward others or for being a "control freak."

Demanding, Acting Spoiled, or Begging

Does your child get whatever he wants or demands? Does he receive unlimited attention and tolerance of his moods? If you are playing a game with him, are you afraid to have him lose? Parents are frequently the last ones to acknowledge that they have a spoiled child. Ask yourself the following four questions.

❏ Do you often feel that your child is too demanding?

❏ Do you often feel guilty that you are giving too much to your child?

❏ Have any other people ever commented to you that your child seems demanding or spoiled?

❏ Do you often "give in" to your child when you don't want to?

If you answer "yes" to two or more of these questions, you are probably raising a child too spoiled or demanding for his own good. Parents raise spoiled, demanding kids for a variety of reasons—everything from fear of rejection, to desire to "buy" a child's love, to continuing a pattern of being spoiled when they were children—but in doing so, you are decidedly *not* preparing your child for the real world.

Frequently, a child is spoiled because of personal issues the parents need to work on. If you recognize this in yourself, you are more than halfway to solving the problem. Read Chapter 10 carefully, as it addresses how to heal yourself so you can be strong and provide your child with what he needs.

The goal is to give your child 100% of what he needs (BASIC parenting) and only about half of what he wants. Again, there is likely to be a struggle for a while. Maintain your resolve, though, and the rewards will be considerable.

Endless Fantasy and Imaginary Friends

Imagination often blossoms around age three. How wonderful this stage of development is. Imagination in a preschooler is a sign that she is developing intellectually and emotionally right on schedule. Imagination begins a child on the road to abstract thinking and learning that symbols and thoughts can have other meanings, a quality important for doing math and reading. Fantasy and make-believe allow children to work through their problems and fears. Peers usually replace their imaginary friends and make-believe thinking around the age your child goes into kindergarten.

A child's disappearance into her fantasy play allows her to accommodate her deepest wishes with imaginary gratification. By recalling the events of her day through fantasy play, she is often able to deal with and process overwhelming and incomprehensible elements of the real world. Your child is able to do and be in her fantasy world what she is unable to do or be in the real world. Fantasy also allows her to work through stressful relationships in ways that don't attract rejection or punishment. For example, she can act out negative feelings toward her parents, siblings, playmates, and caregivers. Your child can practice social skills with her imaginary friend in a non-threatening, self-reliant way. Imaginary friends can help the preschooler deal with missing or absent parents, upsetting friends, and powerful urges. Imaginary friends can provide a companion when lonely, a comfort after a time out, and even a figure to blame for misdeeds.

Don't debate the existence of your child's "friends." The questioning often chases your child's imaginary friends away for a while leaving your preschooler without her "assistant" for dealing with the real world.

Lying and Stealing

The ability to tell the truth or to lie requires an intact moral judgment. This is a complex concept for toddlers and preschoolers. A two-year-old does not yet have a conscience. Developing a conscience requires that parents teach the moral standards of behavior acceptable in the real world. Toddlers and preschoolers have no natural tendencies to "do the right thing." Parents provide the incentives for this behavior with their approval or disapproval. Having a true conscience means that personality monitors come from within without the need of an outside policeman. This internal voice that prohibits behaviors and experiences guilt reactions does not emerge until the fifth or sixth year. In normal healthy children, the conscience does not become a dependable part of a child's personality until he is nine or ten years old (and does not become completely independent of outside authority until late adolescence or early adulthood). In light of this, establishing a pattern of socially acceptable behavior in toddlers is critically important for the eventual establishment of a healthy conscience in later years.

Two- and three-year-olds want their parents' approval so much they are willing to forgo misbehaving when Mommy or Daddy is looking. A child's feeling of being ashamed or being naughty at this age may depend entirely on whether or not he "gets caught." By four or five, a child's conscience begins to emerge and he begins to understand what his parents would want him to do in a particular situation. The child has come to learn what is acceptable to his parents and society through countless situations. Because a conscience is a new aspect of his personality, it does not always work. When a child of four or five fails to pick the path he knows his parents would want him to choose, he is bound to feel guilty. This is a healthy guilt, a guilt uncomfortable enough to motivate the child to select a course of action his parents would prefer. If he chooses this endorsed behavior, he knows it will have the added bonus of not having to feel guilty.

A lie is a willful distortion of the truth. A child's lie is usually motivated by one of four things:

- ❏ To convince you he did or didn't do something.

- ❏ To place the blame on someone else.

- ❏ To get something he wants that he thinks you will deny.

- ❏ To impress others.

Two- and three-year-olds are unable to lie intentionally or plan to deceive another. Until age seven or eight, all children have varying degrees of confusion between what is make-believe and what is true. Preschoolers often apply their concrete and magical thinking patterns to negative thoughts and actions. For example, imagine that your preschooler drew on your wall and you see him with the crayon in his hands. He might respond, "I didn't do it. Charlie (his imaginary friend) did it." The logic that brings him to this response might go something like this: *good people do good things and bad people do bad things. Drawing on the wall is a bad thing. My mommy won't love me if I'm bad. Mommy loves me. So I am a good person. So I didn't do it. Somebody else did it. Charlie is with me a lot—he did it.* Preschoolers need continual reality checks to help teach them about the importance of telling the truth. Don't allow yours to use his imaginary friend to avoid responsibility for his behavior.

Toddlers and preschoolers often have vivid imaginations and conjure up creative stories. Some "lies" happen because the preschooler is upset at something and has resorted to his fantasy world to deal with his stress and tension. He makes up a story partly to cover up his behaviors and partly in his attempt to deal with his stress. This story is often a reflection of how he perceives the world, how he wishes things were, and how he thinks things should be to please you. Be certain not to assume your child is lying (in the adult sense of the word) if he tells tall tales. Accusing him of lying will only add to his stress and force him further into his fantasy world to feel safe. At the same time, don't accept his tall tales as truths. Instead, re-label his tale as an instance of his using his "impressive imagination." This will help him begin to discern in his own mind what is real and made-up.

Don't ever label or think of your preschooler as "a liar." Teach him the important lesson that no matter how bad the behavior is that he might be trying to cover up, that you and society will always view the behavior more harshly if he fabricates a story about it. Explain that in life, when people tell the truth about their mistakes, their consequences are less. For example, say something like, "Honey, you broke Mommy's favorite vase because you were throwing the ball inside when you know you are not allowed to do this. Then you made it worse when you didn't tell me the truth that you broke the vase. Did throwing the ball inside show me the goods? Or did lying about who broke it show me you don't have the goods right now? The goodies you will lose today will be more than if you had told me the truth. If you had told me the truth, you could have kept your ball and gone outside with it. But because you didn't tell me the truth you cannot play with your ball until tomorrow."

Understand that teaching your child not to lie requires countless lessons that you will have to repeat many times until he gets older because he is still learning to discern truth from fantasy.

Stealing in preschoolers is a combination of their "here and now" thinking that says, "If I want it, I take it," and their innocence about real world rules. You must firmly teach your child the rules of society but at the same time never label or think of him as a thief. Stealing at this age is an indication neither of their morals nor of their character because both are still forming.

Deal with stealing in a firm way that teaches your child it is wrong to steal and that he must make amends for this wrong if possible. For example, if you find something in your child's pocket that you know doesn't belong to him, you might say something like, "Honey, I just found this toy and it's not yours. I think it belongs to your preschool's classroom. It is wrong to take things that belong to someone else, so you must return it. Tomorrow I will drive you back to the classroom and you will hand it to your teacher. When you hand it to her you must say you are sorry." Do not stress over this since many children occasionally transgress this way as preschoolers. However, if you find that your child's stealing is increasing or occurs frequently, you may be seeing signs of an emotionally upset child. If firm lessons don't decrease this behavior, you should discuss this with your health care provider.

Not Talking and Shyness

Children learn language skills in a predictable progression. Here are some of the developmentally predictable and key milestones your child should reach as he learns to talk:

- ❏ **15 TO 18 MONTHS:** she will repeat the same word over and over. She may be able to say up to 20 words and understand up to 100. She will often be very chatty.

- ❏ **18 MONTHS TO TWO YEARS:** she may speak in long sentences that are hard to understand. She can make two-word combinations ("Daddy look!" "What's that?"). She is understandable by strangers about 25% of the time.

- ❏ **TWO TO TWO-AND-A-HALF YEARS:** she often asks endless questions of you about "why, what, where, who?" She often loves to sit and read books as she points to words and pictures on the page.

- ❏ **TWO-AND-A-HALF TO THREE YEARS:** she has a several-hundred-word vocabulary and speaks quite well. She is understandable by strangers about 75% of the time.

- ❏ **THREE TO FIVE YEARS:** she can speak well enough to have long conversations with strangers. She is completely intelligible and understandable by strangers 100% of the time. She may make mistakes in grammar ("I singed a song." "My dolly is more bigger than Mary's") that are gradually corrected. At about age 4 she may temporarily go through a mild stuttering stage or have slightly imperfect articulation (e.g., substituting "r's" for "l's"), but this is rarely anything about which to be concerned. If it continues for an extended period of time (more than six months), you should discuss it with your child's health care provider.

As these milestones indicate, your preschooler's language skills will blossom, enabling her to have complex social interactions with people outside of your family. Though strangers can have real conversations with preschoolers, the length, complexity, and content of the conversation will vary depending upon your child's temperament, her feelings of safety in the environment and her life experiences.

If your child is verbal in familiar settings, but quiet in others, relax. Most preschoolers are shy in new situations or with new people. Your child will look to you for reassurance that this new setting is safe for her to feel comfortable and less shy in. Remember to honor your child's temperament.

If your child's shyness is due to her temperament, you will want to follow these tips:

❑ **SHYNESS DECREASES WITH PRACTICE.** Take your child to places where she can meet new people and practice the role-playing you have taught her at home ("Pretend Grandma is a new person you have just met. When I introduce you to a new person, I want you to learn to say, 'Nice to meet you.' Let's practice this."). If you sense your child has really tried hard and is progressing in her ability to handle new situations with even a little less shyness, reward her with praise and/or goodies.

❑ **DON'T CRITICIZE OR LABEL HER** as "your shy child." Remember, when parents label their kids, they often get exactly what they describe.

❏ **ALL CHILDREN HATE BEING IGNORED.** Being ignored is worse than being harped at or criticized. Parents therefore get more of the behaviors they notice and fewer of those they ignore. Make a habit of noticing the times your child talks with others and "ignoring" her shyness.

❏ **REMIND YOURSELF AND YOUR CHILD** that it is OK to be a shy person. The chances are that one of her parents or close family members is also shy. Your shy child will likely never be the "life of the party," but so what?

Help your child warm up slowly to new situations. As an example of how you might help her deal with new transitions, you may want to arrive early at childcare or preschool in order to give her time to adjust. If you get down on your child's level (kneeling or sitting) near her and talk quietly to someone in this new setting, your child will likely feel more comfortable and imitate your behavior.

If you suspect, however, that her "shy" behavior in public is intentional and manipulative, you may need to explain to her that her refusing to be socially appropriate or polite to others is not showing you her goods and will lead to her not receiving the goodie she otherwise would have. For example, imagine your preschooler receives a treat by someone you approve of and refuses to thank the person. You might have to handle the situation by saying, "Honey, I'm going to give you one more chance to tell this nice person 'thank you.' If you aren't polite you will not be able to keep the goodie." Your child will probably wail. But the lesson will not have to be repeated more than once or twice if you hold firm. Do not give in and let her have the treat if she belatedly says, "Thank you . . . Mommy, I say thank you!" This kind of behavior is pure manipulation and needs to be extinguished immediately.

You can tell her, "Honey, when you aren't polite to people as soon as they give you something you aren't showing Mommy your goods so you don't get to keep the goodie. I'm sure next time you will remember to say 'thank you' right away so you will be able to keep the treat."

Picky Eating or Refusing to Eat

It's amazing to me that so many toddler and preschooler households are in conflict over the act of eating. In some families, this relatively simple aspect of life becomes so enmeshed in trauma that it takes on a huge level of importance in the development of the child's personality. Make sure you have your priorities straight—the most important aspect of mealtime for children this age is the time you spend together as a family. If you spend this time talking as a family (keeping the conversation at a level that everyone can understand and participate in) and keep the television off you will accomplish what you need to accomplish at mealtime. Nutritional needs are decidedly secondary at this stage in your child's life.

People carry around some major misconceptions about food. One is that the amount of food you bestow on your child is a reflection of the amount of love you have for him and, conversely, that the amount of food he eats is a reflection of the amount of love he has for you. This is silly and potentially dangerous, as it can burden your child with feelings about food that will have consequences his entire life.

Another false notion is that a child aged two or three needs to eat as much as an infant or young toddler. Children this age normally require significantly less, something that will change dramatically when he reaches age seven. Because your child requires less food, he really may not be hungry when social customs say we should sit down to eat. This doesn't mean he's a picky eater or that he's refusing food to test you. If your child doesn't want to eat at mealtime, don't stress about it. Offer him a *nutritious selection of foods* and let him eat them when he is hungry. If he only wants apple slices for a week, so be it. Just make sure that the seemingly few calories he consumes are nutritious ones and that he doesn't fill up on sugar. Assume that if your child's height-to-weight ratio drops dramatically his health care provider will make you aware of this. Otherwise, learn not to worry about your child's eating habits. If you supplement his daily intake with a basic multivitamin designed for his age, you can rest assured that he is getting the nutrients he needs.

Remember that the main function of family mealtime is the socializing and bonding experience. If your child prefers to eat continuously on the run, but acts politely and appropriately at your family table, then let him honor his own natural biological preferences for eating. Try to include at least one nutritious item on your daily menu that you know your child will like, but don't spend extra time trying to accommodate any difficult (or separate from what the rest of the family is eating) meal preparation request from him. The meal is over when the parents have spent a reasonable amount of time eating their own food and the family has engaged in important family social interaction. Your child's meal is over if he spits or throws his food. If he does this, say to him, "Uh oh, I guess this means you are done eating" as you take his plate away from the table. Don't allow your child to control the meal by not eating when everyone else does and then crying or demanding that his plate not be cleared. The truth is that no child ever starved to death by missing one meal. If you decide that the meal is over, then the formal eating period is over for your child. Don't ever allow your meal table to be filled with coaxing, forcing, threatening, begging, pleading, or cajoling.

Sexual Curiosity and Masturbation

Children have a normal natural curiosity about their (and the opposite sex's) sexual organs. Each age displays characteristic interests or activities. For example:

❏ Two-and-a-half-year-olds frequently show interest in the physical differences between the sexes.

❏ Three-year-olds may verbally express an interest in the different postures used in urinating. Girls may try to pee standing up.

❏ Four-year-olds may be extremely conscious of their navel and private parts when around their parents. They often play the game of "show" with other children their age. They may demand privacy for their bathroom habits, but may want to watch others.

❏ Five-year-olds are often less interested in the physical differences between the sexes. They are more modest with their "privates" and bathroom activities.

Sexual questions should be answered in such a manner that the child has the rudimentary understanding of anatomy and procreation and is proud of his sex and his future sexual role. Don't stress if your child has a misunderstanding of how babies are made or why her sexual organs are different from her sister's. You have plenty of time to straighten her out. Comfort in discussing the topic of sex and its function in creating life is more important than giving your child a complete and accurate understanding at this age. Comfort will help prevent anxiety, shame or guilt about thinking or asking sexual questions. If you discuss sexual content in a comfortable way, your preschooler will feel free to ask you questions when she is puzzled and will develop a desirable attitude about her own body, her own sexual organs, her identification with same-sex friends, and satisfaction with her future sexual role.

Parents should tell their preschoolers that no other person other than health care providers with permission of their parents (including friends and family) has permission to touch them in their "private areas." Tell them as matter-of-factly as you can that if anyone touches them there or expresses a desire to do so to tell you, even if they are asked or have promised not to tell Mommy or Daddy.

Sexual behavior can evoke wildly emotional responses in many parents. Masturbation itself has no direct influence on your child's personality. However, highly charged parental emotional responses to sexual behaviors can have a significant negative affect on the personality of your child. Instilling any form of shame for touching one's genitals risks raising a child whose sexual functions will be crippled as an adult.

Toddlers and preschoolers often naturally enjoy the pleasure of touching their own genitals. Two- and three-year-olds are usually quite casual when their hand strays there and they may be quite oblivious to the presence of others. It is important to teach them the real world rules about this. Your child should learn that some activities are not acceptable in public (such as picking your nose and spitting on the floor) and that masturbating is one of them. Four- and five-year-olds may occasionally touch their genitals in public, but if reminded of the social rules, they usually will refrain from masturbating until they are alone.

If your child appears to engage in masturbating at the expense of other activities (like playing with friends or socializing), or if she appears to touch her genitals repeatedly, particularly in the presence of others, then you may be observing a symptom that deserves further examination and discussion with your child's health care provider. Excessive stress or anxiety can cause youngsters to touch their genitals excessively. Additionally, though rare, some physical conditions increase a child's attention to his genitals. If you fear this is a possibility, get your child checked out and then, if reassured, proceed to consider masturbation as a private activity not worth your notice.

Struggling about Chores

Meaningful chores help build strong character in your child by teaching him that when you work hard, you can get things you want. Kids who are expected to do certain jobs within the family are more likely to grow up responsible and respectful. Chores teach preschoolers how to persevere and struggle with hard work until a job is done satisfactorily and that by contributing to the good of the family they belong to and are loved by that family.

Begin doing housework together when your child is a young toddler. Do things like washing dishes, pulling weeds, sweeping, dusting, etc., while explaining that these are chores that big people have to do as a part of living in the family. Don't mislead him by saying how much fun it is to do these chores. Instead, explain that it is part of the responsibility of being in the family. Focus your attention on the effort your child places on helping you, not the quality of his accomplishments. For example, "Wow, look how hard you are trying to sweep the garage—that really helps Daddy."

When your child reaches an age and ability that he can do a simple chore on his own (age three and older), assign it to him. Remember to explain that big people have to do their work before they can play. Use the important words "as soon as" when talking about chores and then play time. For example, "Honey, feel free to watch your favorite cartoon *as soon as* you change the dog's water dish."

Remember to reward effort rather than quality. Depending upon the age and ability of your child, you may have to redo or correct the quality of his work. Quality is not the key here. If your child understands that doing his chore is his family responsibility, that he must delay his play until he does his work, and if he expends an effort to do it well even though it is a bit of a challenge for him, you can rest assured you are doing an excellent job in fulfilling a part of Principle #3. Don't make the mistake of thinking that your child will ever appreciate having to do chores. If you make it clear, however, that this work is expected of him, you will be amazed at the sense of personal accomplishment he will develop.

Sometimes your child will "forget" to do his chore. You should let him know that if you need to do it instead, you will have to be paid back in time or loss of a goodie. You may want to say something like, "Honey, that's bad news that you forgot to do your chore. This means you didn't show me the goods so I can't give you that goodie because I had to spend the time doing your work. Perhaps if you do something extra for mommy right now you can pay me back for the time I had to spend doing your chore." Make the "payback" activity more difficult or time consuming than his original chore. This teaches him the important adage, "A stitch in time saves nine."

Should your child receive an allowance for his chores? In general, it is better if you don't pay him for those daily chores that are a part of his contribution to the family. This is real world stuff. Do you receive money for all the innumerable chores you do for your family? Allowances are often good, though, for another set of activities beyond his daily chores. This is also real world stuff. When you do extra work, or an extra job on the side, you get more money. You might say, "Honey, the car needs vacuuming and washing. If you work hard and help mommy with this extra work

I'll give you $X so you can buy the toy you wanted." Make sure the money is reasonable (not so much that he can buy almost anything he wants at the end of one week). If you know he wants to purchase a more expensive item, you can help him learn how to save half or all of the money for a certain period. This kind of teaching about real world financing will be invaluable for him.

Toilet Training Woes and Bedwetting

Perhaps no other area of child rearing has greater potential for innocently destroying a healthy parent-child relationship than toilet training improperly. Parents who gauge their success in parenting by how quickly their children are toilet trained are apt to develop destructive anger or resentment in their children. Children who are willing but biologically unable to control their bowels or urine on their parents' timetables frequently suffer great feelings of guilt and inadequacy.

Remember that it is an exceedingly rare thing to see normal teenagers still in diapers. Since this is the case, let go of any preconceived timetables for you child's toilet training. Parents with the best attitude toward body functions are those who wait for their child to ask for help using the toilet instead of their diapers and avoid pressuring, contests of will, and shaming. I am very suspicious of parents who brag to me that their very young child is completely toilet trained. I fear that their child will experience a regression of her toilet training or will demonstrate a fear, anxiety, or other disturbance in another area of her development (e.g. becoming extremely negative about eating). Regression or fear/anxiety is probable in very early-trained kids because their parents almost certainly pressured them into it.

Bowel training is usually much easier and earlier accomplished than urine training. Still, very few children have the biological ability to do this before the age of 18 months. Two-and-a-half-to three-year-olds can be bowel trained quickly. In fact, this is the age when they often begin training themselves anyway. You can begin by predicting the time of your child's defecation and watching for grunting or straining. If you "catch" a bowel movement correctly, you can help your child learn to associate her body feeling of bowel movement with sitting on a toilet the way Mommy and Daddy do. After a while, she will learn to squeeze her anal sphincter muscle until she is fully enthroned on her little potty seat. She will do this partly because of the adoration she receives when she does. Don't overdo the praise, though, or you may find yourself with a child who uses her bowel training to experiment with her newfound independence and ability to displease others.

You may have a child who, after she is bowel trained, begins once again to pass her bowel movements into her underwear (soiling). Soiling may be caused by severe constipation due to a medical problem (rare), a low fiber diet, dehydration, or (most commonly) avoiding bowel movements because they feel painful or as a way to resist toilet training. Have your child evaluated by her health care provider. In most cases, there is no cause for worry. Make sure not to punish your child for these accidents, force her to sit on the potty, or spend excessive amounts of time talking about toilet training. The problem will go away by itself.

Urine training requires more physical maturity than bowel training. Your child may be ready to begin this lesson if she is around her third birthday, is successfully bowel trained, is aware of the feeling of wetness, and can hold her urine for at least a couple of hours. If she awakens from her nap dry, she may be ready. Again, don't stress over this process. You will find yourself in the pleasant position of not having to exert much effort in urine training if you leave the timing up to your child and instead offer her plenty of opportunity to watch the toilet habits of older children and adults. Young preschoolers love to copy others, and if you provide them with a little potty "just like the big one" you will likely have an easy time of your child's urine training.

Night wetting is a problem that is incredibly common in toddlers and preschoolers. Preventing any emotional problems related to bedwetting should be your highest priority. Keep your child in night diapers until she has had at least a couple of weeks awakening to a dry diaper. This accomplishes two things: 1) it avoids the inevitable unpleasant reaction from the parent who comes upon a wet bed and envisions extra work in washing and remaking the bed; and 2) it normalizes the reality that children cannot control their bladder functions any more than you can control how often you toss and turn while you are asleep.

Bedwetting can happen for physical or emotional reasons. Many children under age five wet the bed some nights because of the small capacities of their bladders. If you notice that your child's bedwetting does not lessen in frequency over several months, or your child has achieved nighttime dryness and returned to bedwetting, you may want to have her checked out by your health care provider. Such an exam will help reassure you that your child doesn't have a bladder infection or other anatomical problem that will make it impossible to achieve a consistent dryness through the night.

Once you have ruled out a physical cause, the other likely reason for bedwetting is emotional. A child who experiences upsetting events, or is progressing through a challenging stage of her development often demonstrates her stress through bedwetting. Once again, the best solution (with as little attention or fanfare as possible) is to have her wear night diapers. If your child asks you for additional help, you may want to offer her one of the inexpensive night bladder alarms that will wake her at the first sign of wetness. Only use this device for the older preschooler who expresses her own motivation to learn "to wake up in time." Bedwetting may be an escape valve for her daily stresses, or a minor sign of rebellion for all the restrictions society necessarily places upon preschoolers. Rest assured your child will soon enough find another way to "act out" her frustrations. Remind yourself that her bedwetting is an unconscious symptom of her distress.

Whining and Nagging

Whining and nagging are often pleas for attention. Some kids resort to this because their parents are too busy or too harried to listen to their questions or requests. Kids desperately want to be noticed by their parents and unconsciously, they would rather be yelled at than ignored. Try to be aware of your child's existence and give him more attention. You want to avoid having a child who misbehaves just to be noticed.

Some kids whine and nag because they have learned that the technique works. If this is the case with your child, answer him firmly immediately and if you have decided not to grant his request, *do not* waver. If you waver just once after saying "no," you can be assured that you will need to hold firm at least 50 more times before you can condition your child not to whine. All humans learn through this type of behavior modification: we continue behaviors that have good outcomes and stop those that net us nothing. Remember, though, that even if you "reward" his whining only occasionally, he will continue the behavior in hope of getting what he wants.

Tell your child you've discovered that you simply don't have ears that work when a whining sound comes toward you. Explain that when he whines, for some strange reason the sound comes across as extremely garbled. Tell him, "Honey, I hear a garbled noise but I just can't hear you. I really wish I could because I like to hear what you have to say, but I just can't. I sure hope I don't have to ask you to leave the room. I'll have to do that if the awful garbled noise continues."

The problem behaviors addressed in this chapter have all related to your child's place in the real world. Helping him to navigate through these effectively as a toddler or preschooler will go a long way toward making his later years satisfying and fulfilling.

CHAPTER 8

Attention Deficit Hyperactivity Disorder (AD/HD): Lessening the Symptoms by Using the Three Principles

Most parents have heard of Attention Deficit Hyperactivity Disorder (AD/HD). (Some in the media use the term Attention Deficit Disorder (ADD), but the majority of the medical community uses "AD/HD.") AD/HD is a common neurobiological condition that begins in the preschool age. Even though most children have difficulty at times sitting still, paying attention, or controlling impulsive behavior, the child with AD/HD has great difficulty in one or more of these areas, to the point that the behavior can be quite upsetting to his parents, family, and others.

Up to five percent of all preschool age children probably suffer from this debilitating behavioral condition. If you think your child might be one, it's important for you to have a clear sense of the disorder before I can help you apply the Three Principles.

What Is AD/HD?

AD/HD is a behavioral condition where a child shows "significant deficits in executive functions" and "excessive sensitivity to rejection." *Executive functions* are those tasks that develop normally throughout childhood and are required to be in working order for a person to function well in life. When someone has difficulty in executive functions, she has difficulty with:

❏ The capacity to organize her actions.

❏ The ability to solve problems.

❏ The ability to attain goals.

❏ The ability to employ forethought when applying self-control.

❏ The ability to plan things.

❏ The ability to avoid distractions from her environment.

Children with AD/HD tend to be extremely sensitive and have highly negative reactions to rejection, teasing, and criticism.

AD/HD often occurs with other conditions. Often, young children with AD/HD are delayed in their development, thus making them appear to be less mature and responsible than other kids their age. For example, many health care providers and researchers have found that at least 20-30% of children with AD/HD also have learning disorders or a developmental delay. Twenty-five to forty percent of children with AD/HD also have a form of anxiety or sleep disorders, and as many as 40% also have some sort of depression. AD/HD is also commonly present in children who have serious attachment problems and tic disorders.

Children with AD/HD very often also have Bipolar Disorder (see Appendix #3 for more about Bipolar Disorder). In fact, some studies indicate that if a preschooler has one condition he most likely has or will have the other.

What Causes AD/HD?

AD/HD is a brain nerve problem that prevents the child from properly inhibiting, ignoring or controlling some of her brain impulses or nerve activity. It has many causes, including genetic, brain structural, and mild brain injury (caused by womb problems, early birth, infection, or other environmental factors). About 75% of AD/HD cases can be traced to a "genetic donor"—meaning that 75% of the children have biological relatives who also have this condition. The environment of the pre-birth child and the early life of a newborn is also critical. Exposure during pregnancy to cigarettes or alcohol and many illegal substances increases AD/HD risk dramatically. AD/HD can also occur from direct damage to or diseases of the brain, including attachment disruption (adopted children are especially susceptible to it), fetal drug/alcohol exposure, premature birth, trauma or problems around the birth, significant infant illnesses, early head trauma, etc.

Males and females are about equally affected but females are sometimes less detected or diagnosed because female children and adults tend to be more socialized and culturally more skilled at compensating for their behavioral problems.

Does My Child Have AD/HD?

There are three primary subtypes of AD/HD: AD/HD hyperactive-impulsive type, AD/HD inattentive type, and AD/HD combined type. Many clinicians believe that most preschool children tend to have the hyperactive type and that as they get older the symptoms tend to evolve more toward the impulsive type and eventually predominantly to the inattention type.

Clinicians and medical diagnostic literature look for symptoms in your child that fall into three main behavioral areas—inattention, impulsivity, and hyperactivity. Using the official diagnostic guides, the symptoms must have persisted for more than six months, begin before the age of seven, cause some impairment in more than one setting, cause significant problems in the home and outside the home, and not be explained by another condition or diagnosis.

The predominant symptoms of the AD/HD hyperactive-impulsive type include:

❏ Fidgeting with hands and feet or squirming in a chair.

❏ Having difficulty remaining seated.

❏ Running or climbing around excessively.

❏ Having difficulty being quiet during activities.

❏ Talking incessantly and blurting out answers without listening.

❏ Having difficulty waiting turns and interrupting others.

The predominant symptoms of the AD/HD inattentive type include:

❏ Being careless and not paying close attention to details on work.

❏ Having difficulty staying focused on things.

❏ Appearing not to listen and struggling with instructions.

❏ Losing things and having difficulty organizing things.

❏ Being easily distracted and avoiding tasks that require sustained mental effort.

❑ Being very forgetful.

The child with AD/HD combined type has significant symptoms from both categories.

The most common and important symptoms that clinicians look for when they take a parent's behavioral history of their *preschool* child are:

❑ Motor restlessness.

❑ Aggressiveness.

❑ Tendency to spill things.

❑ Insatiable curiosity.

❑ Being "dangerously daring."

❑ Vigorous and destructive playing.

❑ Being demanding and argumentative.

❑ Being noisy and interrupting often.

❑ Excessive temper tantrums.

❑ Low levels of compliance.

Different clinicians use many different types of tests, screening tools, or behavioral questions to assess AD/HD. The following questions are usually included:

❑ **IS YOUR CHILD EASILY DISTRACTED** by noises, the television, or other people in the room?

❑ **DOES YOUR CHILD HAVE TROUBLE** focusing on things or have trouble doing projects or activities independently (this does *not* include video games or watching TV)?

❑ **DOES YOUR CHILD OFTEN START** things and leave them undone to start other things?

❑ **DOES YOUR CHILD OFTEN ACT** impulsively without thinking about the outcome?

❑ **IS YOUR CHILD IMPATIENT, ALWAYS** climbing and moving around, or accident-prone?

❑ **DO YOU OR OTHERS NOTICE** that your child is excessively noisy, talks too much or too loudly, or is extremely argumentative or demanding?

❑ **DOES YOUR CHILD APPEAR TO** have an inner restlessness, have a short fuse, get angered by petty things, and/or often fly into a rage?

❑ **DOES YOUR CHILD PRESENT** *severe* behavior problems in any of these situations: when playing alone, at meals, when getting dressed, when washing or bathing, when you are on the telephone, when going to bed, when in the car?

❑ **DOES YOUR CHILD PRESENT** *severe* behavior problems in any of these situations: when with other children, when other people are around, when you are visiting others, when in supermarkets, stores, restaurants, or other public places, when with a babysitter?

❑ **IF YOUR CHILD IS ATTENDED** to by other adults, do these adults report that your child shows *severe and frequent* behavior problems in any of these situations: when at preschool, church or day care, with babysitter, with grandparents?

If you find yourself answering many or most of these questions with, "Yes, often," you are likely seeing AD/HD symptoms in your child.

Maybe My Child Will "Grow out of" His Symptoms

This is unlikely. Most children with clear symptoms of AD/HD actually get worse as they get older. It's very difficult raising a child with untreated AD/HD, and much research shows that parental warmth is less toward the untreated child with lots of AD/HD symptoms. About half of older children with untreated or unrecognized AD/HD may go on to have oppositional or conduct disorders that can bring extreme stress and law enforcement problems to a family.

Psychiatric disorders in children can cause lifelong shadows since the suffering disability and family distress leads to additional problems. Older children with untreated AD/HD have a very high incidence of poor school performance, substance abuse, car accidents, strained family and friend relationships, high job turnovers, and general life difficulties. Early and appropriate intervention can avert a downward spiral of bad effects.

How Is AD/HD Treated?

The most effective treatment includes both Specially Targeted Parenting and medication. I realize that many parents abhor the idea of medicating their children and this is fine, particularly at the preschool age. If you want to try to treat your AD/HD child without medication, however, it is critical that you employ Specially Targeted Parenting techniques. Medication, however, rarely works by itself. Remember that pills don't give skills.

The use of medication requires the involvement of a prescribing practitioner. Be certain that you feel comfortable with this health care provider (a nurse practitioner, pediatrician, family physician, child and family psychiatrist, etc.). The initial medication will most likely be either an amphetamine (Dexedrine, Dextrostat, Dexedrine Spansules, Adderall, etc.) or methylphenidate (e.g., Methylin, Ritalin, Metadate ER, Methylin ER, Ritalin SR, Concerta). Both types of medication and some others have an equal chance of helping. Therefore, the choice is somewhat arbitrary though some clinicians prefer one medication over another. Knowing that there are several medications to try, you should work closely with your clinician until you find one that works best for your child's specific physiology. You will begin with the lowest possible dose, and move up gradually until you and your child observe, feel, and see a difference.

Specially Targeted Parenting is a four-step process. The first step involves reading about AD/HD until you no longer blame yourself or your child for the condition. Get rid of the guilt! Think of AD/HD as a condition that requires correction, like discovering your child needs glasses to correct bad vision, a hearing aid to correct poor hearing, or insulin to counteract diabetes. You should prepare for the need for lifelong treatment and support for your child. In addition, since AD/HD is so genetically prevalent, you may want to identify the "genetic donor" and get the appropriate help for that parent or relative.

The second step involves being meticulous and consistent about good health habits for your child. It is essential to stress good nutrition, good sleep habits and ample exercise. AD/HD children do horribly during the day when they eat low protein, high sugar foods, when they haven't slept enough the night before, or when they don't get a regular daily dose of permitted high action motor activity. Additionally, AD/HD children do not adapt well to rapid, unscheduled, unprepared changes—particularly when their day is somewhat chaotic and doesn't follow their predictable routine. Prepare for all changes with plenty of anticipatory explanations. If it is possible to avoid changes to your child's routine, do so.

The third step is to re-read Chapter 4 (Principle #2), since this is the most critical principle for you and your AD/HD child's health and sanity. Use your "one-liner" to stay disengaged emotionally. Delay giving consequences until calm. Make sure both parents carry through on all assigned consequences. Consistently apply the behavioral management techniques you learned with Principle #2 at home and make sure they are applied in the preschool classroom. Try hard to avoid any type of physical punishment for your child's misdeeds. Require that he explain to you "why I did this and what I learned" before he is allowed leave his "time out." Practice forgiveness, patience, and praise. The number of "praise words" you use should be equal to or greater than the number of "discipline words." Remember AD/HD kids tend to have other great characteristics. They tend to be open and warm, have strong verbal skills, be very creative, spontaneous, intuitive, resilient, persistent, have good humor and energy, and have a strong long-term memory.

Principle #1 is also critical. Parenting a child with AD/HD requires a great deal of parent accommodation and must include devoting a considerable amount of attention and time. Your child's symptoms will diminish dramatically if she feels safe, secure, and predictable in her place in the world.

The fourth step is to utilize Principle #3 as effectively as possible, particularly helping your child with his social skills. Primary among this is something I call Affect Attunement. AD/HD kids are often unaware of how others perceive them, including their peers. Therefore, it is essential to keep him based in reality. Your child with AD/HD will fall behind others his age in being able to read others' moods and behaviors correctly. He will misinterpret clues and body language. You must repeatedly (plan to do this for the rest of his childhood) provide social feedback and correction. For example, you will need to have regular interchanges with your child that go something like, "Honey, when you screamed/ grabbed/blurted out just now, how did your friend feel? How did he act? By looking at how he reacted to you, what do you think he was thinking?" Help your child to learn to express his feelings even though he won't necessarily get his way after doing so. When you ask him how he feels, help him learn to respond by saying, "I feel (mad, sad, bad, glad)." Then say back to him, "Thank you for sharing your feelings with me" and follow this with a hug.

AD/HD is a serious condition with serious ramifications. Never underestimate its impact in being able to wreak havoc upon your family if left untreated. Always keep in mind, though, that your AD/HD preschooler is not at fault for her condition. Help her and your parenting partner understand it is not your child's fault that she lacks inhibition, reflection, or self-regulation. Remind yourself that your child is easily distractible and impulsive because she was born with this condition. At the same time, all of you have a responsibility to work toward correcting her symptoms with the help of her relatives, her health care providers, her teachers, and others. If all of you work hard at it, you can lessen the effects of AD/HD.

CHAPTER 9

Applying the Three Principles to Special Circumstances

Life often presents us with painful and stressful realities beyond our control. While watching our children suffer with or through these is difficult, parents who ignore these stressors in order to make their children happy take a path that is detrimental to their child's proper development. Your goal (following Principle #3) must be to help your child deal with his tragedies or troublesome life events in a way that strengthens his character.

Sharing truths about sad occurrences ("Mommy and Daddy are going to stop living with each other." "Grandpa died last night." "We are your real parents, but you also have a biological mother and father." "Daddy lost his job." "Honey, the doctor says you have a really bad illness.") may cause your child to suffer. This is truly a better course, however, than denying these truths or covering them up. Children often have a "sixth sense" about the bad things that happen in a household, and pretending things are normal when they aren't, creates serious problems. For example, assume for a moment that your family faces a huge stress or impending tragedy. If you hide your tears or try to shield your child from pain by shipping her off to a protected environment, she will learn that people leave the ones they love when they need them the most. By showing your emotions honestly, you allow your child to learn to deal with life in a constructive way.

Parenting During Intensely Stressful Life Experiences

Traumatic experiences in early childhood actually affect how the brain organizes itself. Infants and young children require a relatively calm environment for their brains to develop in a predictable fashion. Children's brains develop best when they experience moderate exposure to stress while under the protection of a consistent, available, and safe primary caregiver. Exposure to highly dramatic, sudden, unpredictable, or threatening experiences requires a child's neuroendocrine, immune, and nervous systems to respond in a way that helps him cope. If this response happens too frequently or randomly, it can have a permanent negative impact on him, leaving him with a poor ability to control his emotions and moods or to think and learn properly.

There are many examples of potentially damaging acute or chronic stress. All of these can have an impact on a child's physical, cognitive, social, emotional, or behavioral health and development:

❑ Serious work pressures on one or both parents.

❑ Financial woes or in-law conflicts or problems.

❑ The diagnosis of a chronic illness in the child.

❑ Mental or physical health problems, or drug or alcohol abuse in a parent or close family member.

- ❏ A marriage that was strained before the birth of a child and is now stressed further by typical difficult toddler behaviors.

- ❏ A father who feels shut out or ignored by the mother-and-child relationship or because the mother has no energy for the marriage.

- ❏ A mother who believes the father is not supporting her daily struggles and is jealous of the conflict-free relationship the father has with his young child.

- ❏ Young parents who feel trapped by the loss of independence that comes with the responsibility of child rearing.

- ❏ A working mother who gave up her job for a while and resents the financial strain this causes.

It is not at all surprising for a child to act out the stressors within the family by showing extreme behaviors. These behaviors usually occur during the period after an explosive time, when the home seems at least temporarily peaceful.

The kinds of stress described above are a fact of life in many households. If they exist in yours, your child is not automatically doomed to a difficult life. Here is what you can do to mitigate the effects of chronic or severe stress:

- ❏ **APPLY PRINCIPLE #1 CONSISTENTLY AND DOUBLY.** A kid feels safer and more open about her feelings if he feels that his mother and/or father is "in-tune" with her. Use touch, eye contact, and sensitive warmth liberally. Kids living in stressful home environments need this desperately.

- ❏ **TELL YOUR CHILD ABOUT THE TRAUMATIC OR STRESSFUL EVENT.** If she doesn't have a factual explanation, a child will often "fill in the blanks"—many times with horrible and fantastic inventions that can be worse than the reality. Explain to your child what is going on in a way appropriate to her age. This may cause a great deal of sadness, but it will teach her a meaningful and satisfying way to come to terms with highly emotional events.

❏ **GIVE DETAILS ABOUT THE TRAUMATIC OR STRESSFUL EVENT.** Children benefit from understanding the reality of their lives. Honesty and openness help your child develop trust in you. Give her an age appropriate "who, what, where, why, and how" about the stressful event. Placing the crisis in context and reassuring your child that you will still be there for her helps her cope with the bad experience in a healthy fashion.

❏ **EXPLAIN YOUR EXPRESSIONS OF HIGH EMOTION WITHOUT APOLOGIZING OR BLAMING.** When there is a marital or family conflict, parent or child illness, or a parent-child conflict, your child may see this as a risk to the future availability of her attachment figure. You can help your child's perception of how threatening the stressful events are by explaining why you expressed high emotion (screaming, weeping, rage, etc.) without blaming yourself, her, or others. Explaining the source and context of your high emotions, helps her understand that the expression of emotions does not mean that abandonment is imminent.

❏ **PROVIDE A CONSISTENTLY PREDICTABLE FAMILY ROUTINE.** Your child should have a set pattern and routine to her day including a consistent time for playtime, meals, chores, naps, and bedtime. When her schedule must change, make sure you tell her ahead of time and explain why. She will feel safer if she believes you are in control of her situation.

❏ **GIVE YOUR CHILD CHOICES.** When a child feels out of control due to a stressful situation, offering her a choice of something she can control (what she eats, what she wears, etc.) allows her to feel safer. In addition, allowing her to do something to help out during this difficult time can be very healing as it allows her to follow Principle #3 and learn how to feel satisfaction from helping others. Even if the job has nothing to do with the situation causing the stress, an extra chore will give her the sense that she's contributing during a challenging period in her household.

Single Parenting

A popular TV psychologist recently said three groups of people were the unsung and underappreciated heroes of our time: teachers, nurses, and single moms. I couldn't agree more! Single parenting must be the most difficult job in the world to "do right." A single parent who has a strong healthy available extended family, tons of supportive friends, adequate financial resources to be able to leave work when necessary or desired, and a realistic, non-contentious relationship with the other biological parent can fare very well. Unfortunately, few single parents are blessed with such good fortune. Whether it is because of financial hardship, chronic stress, an absence of a paternal role model, or other reasons, research consistently shows that children raised by single parents are twice as likely to develop a psychiatric illness, commit suicide, or abuse alcohol or drugs when they reach adolescence or adulthood.

This is chilling to consider, but you can take steps to put your child in the best possible position:

❑ **REMEMBER THAT IT TAKES A VILLAGE TO RAISE A CHILD WELL.** Nature designed the human race to have two biological parents who stay together to raise the kids. Parents raising kids *need* a parent partner. Don't think of yourself as inadequate or a failure if you feel overwhelmed. Find a positive support system—

whether it is members of your extended family, your close friends, or even trial living arrangements with other single parents. If this plan is impossible with your life situation, find clubs, congregations, religious groups or others who will help you share your burden. Reach out to find the support you need. You just cannot do this enormous job alone.

❏ **BE SURE YOU READ THE NEXT SECTION.** It contains important tips for protecting your child's self-esteem by properly handling the relationship with his other biological parent. If you are a single parent by design, (never having had a relationship with your child's other biological parent or another partner) reread the previous point and realize that all of us really *do need* help raising children.

Parenting in the Face of Bitter Parental Fighting, Separation, or Divorce

Every year more than a million new children in the nation experience a divorce between their parents. Although many of these children will adapt well, about a quarter of them will develop mental health or adjustment problems (including academic, social, and behavior problems). This is about twice the rate of children from intact families. Bitter parental fighting, domestic violence, separations, and divorces cause serious life stresses with enormous impact on toddlers and preschoolers. Emotional and physical abuse between spouses does incalculable harm to children. Kids exposed to this are sure to show more extreme behaviors.

Research consistently confirms that high parent-child warmth and connection (Principle #1) combined with effective and consistent parental discipline (Principle #2), is the most effective way to parent under these circumstances. Children of divorce have a significantly lower incidence of long-term problems when there is a low level of conflict between the divorced parents. Therefore, parents must try to refrain from fighting in front of their child. Remind each other that, though the two of you may have enormous differences, as loving parents you both owe it to your child to do your best to present yourselves as a cooperative unit. It is *much healthier* for your child to receive consistent discipline from parents who are on the same page (or at least relatively so).

Parents who are fighting, separating, or are already divorced must understand three basic realities with regard to their children:

❏ The child usually perceives parental discord as a threat to the accessibility to his attachment figure. This leads to feelings of anger, fear, or sadness.

❏ The child initially interprets everything negative related to his parents as his fault and proof that he is a bad child. Suzie will think that her parents are fighting because she lost her sweater at preschool. Jim will blame himself that his parents are getting a divorce because he didn't always remember to feed the dog.

❏ The child views himself as attached, devoted, and loyal to both parents, regardless of the relative strength of the character of one parent over the other.

When the fighting is serious, is leading to a separation, or has ended in divorce, you and your spouse must talk individually with your child and give him these four messages:

❏ That both you and your spouse are trying or tried hard to make the marriage work.

❏ That the fighting between you and your spouse is *not* his fault —it's what adults sometimes do when they are married or living together.

❏ That you and your spouse still love him.

❑ That regardless of what happens, you and your child's other parent will make sure to take care of him.

Share these four messages with your child continually. Repetition is essential.

Each parent often believes that the other is more to blame for conflict in or dissolution of the relationship. Sometimes this is actually the case. This does not, however, give the "healthier" parent permission to criticize the more troubled parent. I ask my clients to envision that their child views himself as having a dotted line down the middle of his front. He sees his right half as his mom and his left as his dad. If one partner insults or degrades the other one in front of the child, the child's self-image and sense of safety suffers dramatically.

The goal for each child is to learn how to view each of his parents clearly and honestly, without a contaminated emotional overlay. Kids who are exposed to highly destructive anger or contempt from one parent toward the other are at high risk for viewing one or both of their parents using fantasy (blind unrealistic adoration), denial, or defensiveness toward the maligned or absent parent. Young kids will automatically defend (either openly or to themselves) the other parent regardless of the character merits of each child's parents. Don't be fooled into thinking that your child is not thinking about or feeling this loyalty if he says things like, "I don't like Daddy" or, "Mommy is so mean to me" or, "I like you better than Daddy" or, "I don't want to go to Mommy's house." Kids oftentimes feel unable to share all of their feelings because they desperately want to please the parent they are with at the time and they don't like hurting either one.

So what should you do if you are the "healthier" parent? You must refrain from labeling, particularly when you are emotionally charged. If your parenting partner has traits or behaviors that you believe your child should have explained to him, do the explaining when you are calm and rational. Suppose your child's other parent is in jail, uses drugs, or has just walked out on the family. Do not yell descriptors about your spouse or ex in front of your child right after he has let you down or stressed you ("That man is a worthless bum" or, "She is such a useless excuse for a mother"). Instead, when you are calmer, say something like, "Honey, there are many great things about your father. He loves you a ton, but sometimes he makes bad choices like drinking too much beer which makes him difficult for me to deal with." The key is to avoid implying that your spouse's *very being and soul* is worthless; instead clarify (if true) that your spouse makes bad decisions at times.

Suppose your spouse or "ex" has a terribly unhealthy behavior trait and you want your child to be able to see the behavior correctly without feeling defensive, guilty or pity for "the other half of him." Let's assume your child's other parent regularly promises visits or phone calls and then fails to show up. If you scream insults about the other parent ("I am so sick and tired of him letting you down all the time—he is mean and cruel and I hate him for doing that to you!") your child will feel your energy, believe the message that half of him is "mean and cruel," and will likely feel defensive about his other parent. A much better approach is to first calm down and then say, "Honey, I fell in love with your dad many years ago because there are many good things about him and in his core he is a good man. However, one behavior he chooses to do that is difficult for us is making promises and then breaking them. You are different in many ways from both of us—because you are becoming your own person. I'll bet you won't choose to break promises because you are learning how much it hurts another person."

Conversely, describing the other parent with an incorrect cheeriness or positive slant does your child no favors either. Telling your child, "Your father is so wonderful," or, "We are just one big happy family" when he experiences tons of contentious fighting or anger screws up your child in another way. Your child sees the turmoil but hears a different description. He will invariably believe that he cannot trust his own emotions and will learn to discount his own messages and feelings.

Clear unemotional descriptions will help him understand why difficult things happen to him without his believing that he is to blame and that he has to defend part of himself to you or others. Always remember that when your child hears descriptors from one parent about the other parent he will tend to believe that he holds those traits too (unless you properly frame the traits for him). If there are qualities that you do not like in your partner that do not have an impact on your child, try to keep these to yourself. Framing the reality of the other parent's choices for his behavior clearly and unemotionally without unfair labeling (no matter how difficult the information) is the healthiest and most loving thing you can do for your child under these circumstances.

Parenting When There Are Stepparents Involved

Members within a stepfamily feel many stressors. Stepmothers commonly feel used, stepfathers commonly feel like outsiders, stepchildren commonly feel torn and alone, the new marital partners commonly feel time-conflicted between their children and their new relationship, and non-custodial parents commonly feel a profound loss of power over their biological child's life and direction. Additionally, the new marriage partners face ghosts from their previous marriage and there is commonly contentiousness between the stepmother and ex-wife. Because both parents are likely coming from a failed first marriage, and the children invariably are traumatized from the loss of their primary family, statistically certain mental health issues (depression, anxiety, addictive disorders, adjustment problems, etc.) are more prevalent in the children from stepfamilies.

Stepfamilies go through a predictable set of steps in their development:

- ❏ In the first stage, children often fantasize about things being the way they were before their parents divorced. The stepparent often becomes the target of strong feelings from the child because of this.

- ❏ In the second stage, parents begin to look honestly at the various needs of their biological and stepchildren and negotiate a way for things to go as smoothly as possible.

- ❏ In the third stage, a true new family history begins to form among the members. The issues around stepparenting may still arise, but they no longer threaten the couple or stepparent-stepchild relationships.

The following points will help you and your child develop in a healthy way when you are involved in a stepparenting situation:

- ❏ **DON'T EXPECT INSTANT LOVE BETWEEN A CHILD AND HIS NEW STEP-PARENT.** All involved parents must accept the reality that their children have more "parents" now and thus the nurturing is no longer identical to that possible in a traditional family. Your child may not be willing to move toward loving her new stepparent and this can feel very hurtful to the stepparent who wants to bond with the stepchild. Respond to this with patience and understanding.

- ❏ **ALLOW YOUR CHILD TIME TO GRIEVE THE LOSS OF HER BIOLOGICAL PARENTS' HOME.** Anticipate that your child will need plenty of time to be very sad about her many losses (losing availability to you because of the new marriage, loss of dreams about a "normal" family, losses related to moving, etc.) and will need to learn to cope with the new realities of her life. Don't take it personally if your child appears to be sullen or withdrawn as she slowly adjusts. Allow the child to have pictures and memories of her other parent. Your child will likely achieve a new balance and acceptance of her life and become emotionally stable again— even if it takes several years.

❏ **DO NOT ALLOW THE TERM "WICKED STEPMOTHER" OR OTHER NEGATIVE TERMS TO BE USED ABOUT ANY PARENT.** Try not to use negative terminology when referring to any of the parents in your child's new extended family. Don't use damaging labels even if you are tempted. Remember that while you may not have much respect or use for one or more of the members of your child's new reality, it doesn't help your child to confuse her with insults against people she has to spend time with. Staying neutral and unemotional while helping your child understand the various idiosyncrasies of the people involved will help your child learn to see people clearly without invoking a request for loyalty.

❏ **HONOR AND PROMOTE THE RELATIONSHIP BETWEEN A CHILD AND HER BIOLOGICAL PARENTS.** Rid yourself of the bitterness toward the other parent that often exists after a divorce. Remind yourself that presumably at one time you really loved this other person and that your child still does love him or her. Even if your new spouse is clearly more balanced or "good for the child," remember that the child's primary loyalties are to her biological parents. Research shows that children adjust best to their stepfamily when they have easy and frequent access to both parents. Except in tragic situations involving biological parent abuse, every parent should promote easy and frequent access to the other biological parent. If a biological parent exists only in memory and not reality, the child often will create and form new memories based upon fantasy and sainthood—a terribly unrealistic burden to carry while learning to deal honestly with life.

❏ **REMEMBER THAT WITH VISITATION** *arrangements (non-cohabitating stepfamilies) it can take even longer to bond.* If a child is only with you on the weekends or summer, you must understand that the normal process of developing a new family will take even longer to form. You must be even more patient for the relationships to become positive. Even though you may love your new partner immensely, don't expect your child to fall in love with her new stepparent. If you expect this, you are likely to become frustrated and angry when this doesn't happen. Allow time and creative solutions for developing close relationships between the new stepparent, step-grandparents, stepsiblings, step-aunts and -uncles, step-cousins, and all the other step-in-laws.

❏ **THE PARAMETERS FOR PRINCIPLE #2 SHOULD BE DEVELOPED MUTU-ALLY BY THE BIOLOGICAL PARENTS.** Nothing approaches a more potentially volatile and destructive situation than the area of discipline. The biological parent must reinforce the fact that both biological parents have established the consequences and "goods for goodies" rules, and that the stepparents have their blessing when carrying out these rules.

❏ **TRY TO HONOR THE DIFFERENCES BETWEEN THE FAMILIES.** Just because you and your new spouse parent differently from your child's "other family" doesn't mean that either is wrong—just different. Ask yourself if the differences in parenting style do your child any harm. For example, if your child is allowed to stay up later, wear different clothes, and eat different foods at her "other home," are these really a problem? If not, don't react. Even though it's easier on a child if the safety and household rules are consistent, your child is perfectly capable of understanding that the different households do things differently.

❑ **DON'T EXPECT THAT A NEW BIOLOGICAL CHILD BETWEEN THE TWO NEW PARTNERS WILL "SOLVE" ANY PROBLEMS THAT ARISE.** Mutual children can complicate the already difficult interpersonal dynamics between existing stepparents and stepchildren. Jealousies and resentment between a mutual child and stepsiblings can be complex and unending.

❑ **SEEK OUTSIDE COUNSEL TO HELP PREVENT LEGAL AND FINANCIAL CONFLICTS WITH THE NEW FAMILY.** Legal experts in stepfamily issues can help you address the complicated potential problems such as custody, visitation, adoption, child support, inheritance, and federal benefits. Many stepfamilies need outside professional help and planning utilizing sensitive lawyers and financial advisors to avoid the inevitable money issues that can emerge to complicate the stepfamily relationships.

Adoptive Parenting

Parenting an adopted child can be a wonderful experience, but it is almost always more difficult than parenting one's own biological children. In addition to the problems, challenges, and stresses inherent in raising a child, there are additional potential complications such as unknown genetic influences, the reality of the biological parents' existence, grief and loss related to the adoptive experience for both the child (over losing his biological parents) and the parents (over giving up the dreams of a biological child), and loyalty concerns.

Two key factors in the degree of difficulty in parenting an adopted child are the child's age at adoption and the environment and quality of his attachment to prior caregivers. Adopted children (particularly those with a history of contentious or late removal from the biological parents, a long stay in an orphanage, or a history of many prior living situations) comprise a large percentage of children, adolescents, and adults with subsequent psychiatric illnesses. Among the most common of these illnesses are Reactive Attachment Disorder, Bipolar Disorder, Attention Deficit Hyperactivity Disorder, Oppositional Defiant Disorder, Conduct Disorder, serious mood disorders, and addictive disorders.

Each year, Americans adopt nearly 20,000 children from a variety of countries around the world. Many of these children have spent their early weeks, months, and years in orphanages. These children are more likely to have suffered varying degrees of emotional deprivation, poor health and nutritional care, neglect, trauma, and loss. Research clearly shows that there is a strong correlation between the length of stay in an orphanage and subsequent developmental delays and mental health problems.

Clearly, parenting under these circumstances requires extra diligence. Adoptive parents should:

❏ **UTILIZE PRINCIPLE #1 INTENSELY AND CONSISTENTLY.** Holding, touching, and eye contact are critical in these situations. Newly adopted toddlers and preschoolers frequently show signs of withdrawal from affection, intense anger or rage, fear, and sadness. When you see these signs, hold your child gently but firmly through his intense emotion until he quiets down. Do this without interruption even if it takes an hour or more. He needs to know that he can express his intense emotions and that you will still be there for him. Don't stop holding him even though he may wail and thrash against you—he is actually testing you to be certain you will stay with him no matter how horrid he acts. Once his rage passes, he will settle down into your arms, in a love-filled snuggle. Your patience will be rewarded, as this time is one of the sweetest feelings you will have. If your child's rages never seem to stop and he has been in an orphanage or foster home or has a history of abuse, you may need to obtain professional help to assist you in this attachment process.

❏ **ALLOW YOUR CHILD TIME TO WORK THROUGH AND GRIEVE HIS LOSS.** Adoption can trigger feelings of abandonment in a child—after all, from his perspective his first parents, regardless of the reason, abandoned him. No matter how little time your child spent with his biological parents, he still has had to sever his primary connection. All parents of newborn adoptees must anticipate that their infant needs to "grieve" the loss of the mother within whose body he spent his first nine months. If you permit some of the early signs of grieving (more intense crying, listlessness, etc.), you can minimize the disruption that comes from changing parents. Your child, regardless of his age, may go through stages of shock, anger, withdrawal, sadness, and despair before finally achieving a sense of acceptance of his new environment.

❏ **TALK TO YOUR CHILD ABOUT ADOPTION**—never *keep it a secret.* Secrets destroy his trust in you because he will either sense something (no matter how deep and unconscious) or he will discover this secret from someone else. In either situation, he will feel betrayed. Don't let this happen. Tell him the moment he is in your arms, even if you think he is too young to understand. Say something like, "Honey, though you didn't grow in my tummy you grew in my heart. You have different biological parents, but we will always be your *real* parents because we will love you and raise you. Your biological parents loved you too in their own way, and we are so thrilled they gave you life so you can continue to grow in our hearts and home. We will love you forever." If you adopt a child in infancy, he should never be able to remember when he learned he was adopted—it should simply be something he has always known.

❏ **READ TO YOUR CHILD ABOUT ADOPTION.** There are many wonderful books about adoption available for young children. Choose books that most clearly match your child's history and past. As you read the book, you can add your child's information among the pages to personalize the story for him. This can become a treasured memory.

Parenting after a Death

Death is a natural part of life. If you attempt to prevent your child from feeling grief, you are violating Principle #3. Children often become aware of death without our even realizing it. They see dead animals alongside the road, they see death on TV, they hear about it in fairy tales. Your child is entitled to experience grief when someone in her life dies (his pet, his grandparent, etc.). Feeling loss is a human emotion you should not deprive her from having. Allowing her to mourn dead pets fully, for example, allows her to learn how to deal with loss. A child shielded from the sadness and grief of life often grows up presenting emotional facades to the world because she learned that intense sadness is an impermissible emotion. Try not to get in the way of her grieving. Cry and feel the hurt along with her.

Families who have lost a close member often feel grief so intensely that they're emotionally unavailable to one another. Parents may erect emotional walls against the horrendous pain they feel. This prevents them from being able to interact genuinely with others in the household. These walls can prevent a parent from maintaining an attachment with her young child. Children from families struck by tragedy are often afraid to talk about their

feelings and instead show them through their behaviors. This acting out often increases the distance from their parents under these
trying circumstances.

Giving your child a realistic perspective on death often helps.
Here are the steps you should take:

❏ **TELL CHILDREN ABOUT DIFFICULT SUBJECTS OR EVENTS AHEAD OF TIME
(IF POSSIBLE) OR AS THEY HAPPEN.** You may want to protect your
child from harsh realities, but remember, hard times are part
of life, and trying to shield her from the realities of life is not
being true to Principle #3. Tell your child the age appropriate
truth about the impending bad news so she can psychologically
prepare for and understand what is happening to her. This
knowledge provides her with a sense of control and helps diminish her feelings of fear, anxiety, terror, and abandonment.

❏ **ANSWER ALL QUESTIONS HONESTLY TO AN AGE APPROPRIATE LEVEL.** If
you have to share bad news like the serious illness or death of
a close family member, let your child ask questions. Answer
these while keeping in mind that the real question on her mind
is, "Will I still be safe or does this mean I am being abandoned,
deserted, or rejected?" If you don't reassure your child that she
will remain safe, she will assume the worst and assume that she
is somehow at fault. In talking about death, remember that
your toddler or preschooler is a concrete thinker. Remind her
of the person who died by showing her a picture and then talking about how you both will always remember the good times
with this person.

❏ **ALLOW YOUR CHILD TO EMOTE.** If your child greets the bad news
with wails, pleading, and crying, she is responding normally.
Use this opportunity to comfort her and be close to her. Let
her emote all she wants to and let her express her true feelings.

She needs to cry in your arms while being comforted. She will gain strength from this. Draw your child closer to you while you grieve, so you can share the grief together and obtain comfort from the closeness between the two of you. Allow yourself total one-on-one time with your child before you reenter the chaos and preoccupying stress inherent with a death. This will lessen her fears of abandonment.

❏ **SEEK COUNSEL FOR YOURSELF IF YOU HAVE TROUBLE WATCHING THE EXPRESSION OF GRIEF IN YOUR CHILD.** Parents can sometimes feel angry (even filled with rage or fear) when their children cry uncontrollably or act in ways they feel powerless to stop. These parents are likely having their own early subconscious memories stirred . . . memories of their own terror at feeling lost or abandoned or left in a huge world without the comfort they so desperately wanted but did not adequately receive. If you are having an intense emotional reaction to your child's display of tears or sadness, read the next chapter for ideas on how to help deal with these emotions.

CHAPTER 10

Healing Your "Self"

Do you feel that your intense negative emotions sometimes get the best of you? One of the best benefits to being a parent is that you can heal yourself in the process of raising your child. You may have noticed aspects of your parenting that upset you because they remind you of painful experiences from your own childhood. This is very common. As parents we tend to re-create in adulthood the same dynamics and emotional climate we experienced as a child because humans are drawn toward the familiar. Adults who come from chaotic homes filled with alcoholism or a sense of helplessness often marry a partner with similar characteristics and repeat the pattern. Adults who felt emotionally abandoned as children frequently create adult relationships that leave them feeling abandoned because this is the feeling they are most familiar with and, ironically, most comfortable with.

We also tend to copy the familiar. Parenting behaviors are to some degree preprogrammed in us. While parents of a new infant often automatically feel a strong urge to behave in certain predictable ways—like cradling their infant when he cries and keeping him warm, protected, and fed—these automatic parenting behaviors are soon replaced by the behaviors observed from one's own parents. If there were serious flaws in the way you were parented, this can lead to the repetition of these harmful techniques. Before you can break this pattern, you need to make an honest assessment of your childhood.

The first step to addressing this is understanding your negative emotions, where they come from, and how to begin to help yourself heal and release the binds of your past.

Healthy and Unhealthy Anger

Parental anger is a normal event because children bring to the family environment a range of aggravations including turmoil, disorder, loss of parental privacy, and loss of personal time. This anger can be surprisingly intense, though, when it brings up unwanted memories from your own childhood. Adults who experienced insecure attachments or chaotic and stressful homes in their childhood often have frequent feelings of deep anger as parents.

Not all anger is unhealthy. It can, in fact, reestablish and strengthen a soothing attachment connection between two people. For example, anger can be functional when it motivates family members to work on their problems. However, when the anger is continuous and intense, this is unhealthy and can cause an attachment relationship to become more distant and lead to running resentment.

Emotions in adults are often the product of how they were cared for as small children and the type of environment in which they were raised. The attachment patterns we experienced as children correlate with the emotional patterns we feel and express as adults. If your experience with anger and related strong feelings toward your child has motivated you to seek help, this healthy action will help improve your relationship with your child and even perhaps with your own parents and spouse.

Adult Feelings of Intense Anger— A Process of Healing

The good news is that adults with a less-than-perfect childhood can learn how to examine their past realistically and break the pattern and heal. You can learn how and why you are "triggered." If you can put a voice to your emotions, you'll feel less need to act them out.

Some people go to great lengths to avoid looking honestly at their past. These include:

❑ Denying or stifling feelings ("My childhood was fine").

❑ Intellectualizing emotions instead of feeling some of what we felt as a child ("Things may have been tough but my parents did the best they could and I am fine").

❑ Using a numbing agent like alcohol, drugs, or cigarettes to help cover up the pain.

❑ Being fearful about expressing feelings and emotions ("God or my parents will be furious if I think negative thoughts about my parents").

❑ Feeling that you must protect your parents from your anger ("If I express anger, even if I only write about it or talk to others about it, my parents won't love me").

❑ Attacking the source that suggests you look at your childhood ("You're wrong for suggesting that how my parents raised me may be the cause of my anger—they did nothing wrong").

❑ Trivializing emotions you have deep within you ("I just decided one day to forgive my parents so now it's no longer an issue").

❑ Believing that there is something wrong with a person who shows their emotions ("I'm an adult—I should be able to cope with whatever I experienced as a child").

Remember, though, that it takes more emotional energy to hide from your past than it does to examine your childhood honestly and grieve your losses or traumas. Parents who refuse to look honestly at their painful pasts suffer greatly—and their suffering spills over to their kids and spouses. Parents who feel and grieve honest emotions about their past are released from anger's hold and can live more peacefully.

Think of it this way: *admit it or repeat it.*

Achieving a Sense of "Earned Security"

Making the decision to rid yourself of some of your "old baggage" so you will feel less triggered and angry is an enormous accomplishment in itself. If you are ready to make that decision, the following three steps will help you become more aware of yourself so you can get rid of the intense emotions that are running (and ruining) your life as a parent. Through these you can achieve a sense of "earned security" that will allow you to feel calmer, happier, and more content with your relationships.

❑ **STEP ONE: BECOME MORE AWARE OF YOURSELF AND YOUR CHILDHOOD.**
The importance of self-awareness cannot be overstated. Everything you experienced as a child is still in you, and the more you can remember, the less your painful memories will control you. Parents who are unaware of their own backgrounds respond badly to qualities they see in their children that remind them of

things they don't like or don't accept in themselves. As you become aware of these things, you will find that you have an added tolerance and love for yourself and your child.

Research shows that a parent's ability to think comprehensively and accurately about her own childhood attachment experiences is essential to obtaining a sense of "earned security" in your attachment with your loved ones. Having a child allows you the chance to "do your childhood over" and heal from some of the painful emotions you may have experienced back then. As you become more aware of your history and the source of your emotions you can provide your child with the emotional security and feelings of safety (Principle #1) that you may have missed when you were a child.

❏ **STEP TWO: WRITE YOUR LIFE STORY TO BECOME MORE SELF-AWARE.**
Write a little about your early childhood memories. I call this your Life Story. The value of completing your Life Story is that it increases your awareness of and helps you to understand patterns from your past so you can learn how these patterns relate to your current emotional triggers. Find time by yourself (you will need at least an hour) to think about the following prompts. Allow yourself to feel the feelings and emotions that emerge as you write.

➤ List at least five descriptive words or phrases about your mother (or the female in your life who raised you when you were birth through age five). For example, was she warm, cold, happy, sad, open, secretive, gentle, harsh, stern, playful, kind, mean, sedate, adventurous, dependent, independent, forgiving, critical, accepting, a gentle disciplinarian, a harsh disciplinarian, etc.? Write down at least one memory per descriptive phrase that validates each of the descriptions you chose.

➤ List at least five descriptive words or phrases about your father (or the male in your life who raised you when you were birth through age five). For example, was he warm, cold, happy, sad, open, secretive, gentle, harsh, stern, playful, kind, mean, sedate, adventurous, dependent, independent, forgiving, critical, accepting, a gentle disciplinarian, a harsh disciplinarian, etc.? Write down at least one memory per descriptive phrase that validates each of the descriptions you chose.

➤ List five descriptive words or phrases to describe yourself when you were between the ages five and ten. For example, were you happy, sad, afraid, trusting, shy, wild, rebellious, obedient, reserved, affectionate, independent, dependent, a loner, anxious, fearful, upset, etc.? Write down at least one memory that validates each of the descriptions you chose.

➤ How would you have finished this sentence when you were between the ages five and ten: "Dads are _____."?

➤ How would you have finished this sentence when you were between the ages five and ten: "Moms are _____."?

❑ **STEP THREE: SHARE YOUR LIFE STORY WITH A SAFE AND SUPPORTIVE IMPORTANT PERSON IN YOUR LIFE.** After you have finished your Life Story ask your spouse, partner, or trusted friend if you can talk sometime about what you have written. You will heal through connecting with this trusted adult. Using your words to express your feelings to your loved one's or trusted friend's eyes is a very healing connection.

You are asking a trusted adult to do for you what a good, mature, loving parent would do. If you can do this with the other parent to your child, that would be ideal, though not essential. Most important is that your adult listening partner be able to listen quietly and be supportive for you, even when you feel filled with emotion. Plan to talk when you will have at least two hours of private uninterrupted time. Ask that your listening partner use lots of direct eye contact and gentle, close, non-sexual, supportive touch as you explain your responses and tell your life story.

Bringing your painful memories out in the open diffuses the negative energy within you and lessens the rage. Talking about your painful past with an accepting person always lessens the pain because sharing with a safe person releases some of the negative energy stored and trapped within your head so you will feel better. It has taken a huge amount of energy to suppress your old memories. When you release them, you will likely cry and find much relief. Verbally sharing your past in a safe place helps you let go of it and allows you to become the person you want to be.

Don't expect to get everything on the table in one session. Understanding yourself takes lots of time. You will discover new emotions each time you retell your story. You will likely only examine those painful parts of your childhood that you can handle for the moment. Ask that your trusted spouse, partner or friend not push you to talk about more than you are comfortable revealing at any one juncture.

If you feel extremely uncomfortable with this, you may want to consider talking to a religious guide or professional coach/counselor/therapist. It is a sign of health to admit you want professional help. The healthiest people are the ones who admit at one time or another in their lives that they can use some assistance from a skilled mental health professional. The most mentally unhealthy people are the ones who are most likely to refuse help throughout their adult life. The profes-

sional you choose must be someone you feel safe with immediately—it is *not* the person with the "right credentials" or the
"right reputation." Trust yourself and your gut feelings.

Emergency Anger Management Skills

Until you are well along on your journey to achieving "earned
security," you will most likely need to use certain tricks to help
you handle the intense emotion of anger. As you get more in
touch with your emotions and find yourself less triggered by
problem behaviors in your child, you will find it less necessary
to use these anger management techniques. These techniques
will do little to prevent the intense feelings of anger that may
well up within you (the steps in the previous section will help you
there). Listed below are stopgap measures to help you avoid letting your anger disrupt your ability to use the Three Parenting
Principles:

❏ **NEVER GIVE A PARENTING CORRECTION OR CONSEQUENCE WHEN YOU
ARE ANGRY.** The first thing you must do is to take yourself away
from the situation. Be certain your child is in a safe place and
then leave. Tell your child "I am quite angry right now and I
will return when I feel calmer." Remember that the most beau-
tiful thing about silence and leaving the room when you feel
triggered is that you never have to take anything back. Remember to use your one-liners constantly. If you need to use
your favorite one-liner a hundred times a day that is fine. Your
child will view this as a powerful response and an indication
that you take his behavior seriously.

❏ **NEVER USE PHYSICAL PUNISHMENT.** If you feel that you might
strike your child, use your one-liner, and exit the situation *immediately*. Find a quiet spot and rethink what just happened.

❏ **BREATHE.** Now that you are safely away from your loved one, breathe as deeply as you can 10 times. The extra oxygen you send to your brain will help you calm down and enable you to think more clearly. Talk to yourself and say something like the following: "I feel furious but my intense anger is OK and I should not feel guilty about having these feelings." Remember that feelings are not the same as actions. Remind yourself that it is perfectly OK to *feel* these emotions while it is not OK to *act out* these feelings. *Thinking horrible thoughts is completely different from doing horrible things. What you do with your angry thoughts makes all the difference.*

❏ **ACKNOWLEDGE YOUR FEELINGS OF EXTREME ANGER.** The action of verbalization acts like the valve on a pressure cooker. Describe how you feel out loud. Talk to yourself—mirrors in a private bathroom work wonders. Learn to accept intense feelings and thoughts within yourself while reassuring yourself that you are perfectly capable of not acting on those feelings.

❏ **RECOGNIZE THAT THE INTENSITY OF YOUR EMOTIONS RIGHT NOW RELATE MORE TO YOUR PAST THAN TO THE BEHAVIORS OF YOUR CHILD.** Repeat the following phrase in your head: "Yes, my child has done something wrong, but I am this angry because of *my* old stuff." Remember that when your toddler or preschooler misbehaves and you feel incredibly angry, it is likely that your child has just "triggered" you to feel old emotions buried deep within you. It is extremely unlikely that your child's behavior is so terrible that he deserves that much anger from you. This "cognitive reframing" of the event will give you a further opportunity to calm down and allow you to think about how your child's behavior has just reminded you of your own pain and emotions. Remind yourself that as you continue to share your Life Story with a trusted friend you will heal and feel less anger.

❑ **REMIND YOURSELF THAT IT'S OK TO HAVE AMBIVALENT FEELINGS TO-WARD LOVED ONES.** Knowing that it is acceptable to feel both hatred and love at different moments toward loved ones is an important thing for all humans to acknowledge. Remember that there can only be moments of intense hatred where there is intense love. This will help calm you down when you feel out of control. For example, it's OK that your child said, "I hate you" when you denied him something. Although this angers you and makes you feel rejected or abandoned, remind yourself that kids and adults can hold these feelings temporarily toward a loved one without it being a true attachment injury. Understand that your goal is to help your child label and accept his emotions without having this behavior manipulate you into trying to make him happy again.

❑ **WAIT UNTIL YOU FEEL CALM AND CENTERED BEFORE THINKING ABOUT YOUR CHILD'S MISBEHAVIOR AND WHAT GOODIES YOU WILL DENY.** At this point, you can feel safe and return to your child. Share your Principle #2 consequence with your child as a calmly considered response to his behavior. Remember, no matter how endearing or penitent your child now appears, it is important that you carry through on your decision. Principle #2 gives you guidance on how to wait to react so your parental response avoids hurting, insulting, demeaning, or inspiring feelings of rage and revenge in your child while also teaching him that his behavior was inappropriate and comes with consequences.

❑ **REMEMBER THAT INTENSE FEELINGS AND EMOTIONS ARE WORSENED BY FATIGUE OR STRESS BROUGHT ON BY LIFE EVENTS THAT CAN HAVE LITTLE TO DO WITH YOUR CHILD.** Don't shortchange health habits as an important way to avoid getting angry with your loved ones. Take regular exercise breaks to relieve irritability and tension. Eat meals on time—both yours and your kid's patience and tempers become short with a low blood sugar. Avoid too much caffeine and get enough sleep.

❏ **REMEMBER THAT PERFECTLY NORMAL CHILDREN AND ADULTS CAN HAVE AND SHARE STRONG EMOTIONS AT TIMES.** Just because your child is defiant, screams at you, or engages you in a power struggle doesn't mean that either of you is disturbed. If you and your child have a healthy, securely attached relationship, an occasional strong "unhealthy" knee-jerk verbal reaction from you will not harm him. In fact, it's healthy for him to see a broad variety of emotions in you. In the heat of the battle, even the best parents can lose their cool and say and do things from a gut level of response. Just be sure not to make a habit of delivering "unhealthy" responses. Regular and frequent parent responses of ridicule, intense anger, or disgust are damaging to a kid's self-concept (see Appendix #4 for a list of unhealthy responses that can be damaging to your child).

The goal for parents then is to learn to express their natural feelings of anger without harming their children physically or emotionally. Looking honestly at your life allows you to see things for what they are. Honestly examining your own childhood can allow for emotional maturity, a lessening of fear, a greater ability to control your emotions, and an ability to feel "triggered" far less often.

What Is More Important for a Child, Nature or Nurture?

The Classic Nature versus Nurture Debate

Gwen's parents are convinced that her problem behaviors are because "she looks and acts just like her aunt." Tom's parents wonder if his temper tantrums are because his mom was depressed during the first few years of his life. You may wonder if your toddler or preschooler's difficult behaviors are worse because "the problem runs in the family" or because "something bad happened" to him when he was young. What plays a more important role in how your child turns out, the gene or the scene? This is the classic "nature versus nurture" debate. When we think of a child's "nature," we think of his biological, genetic, and cellular makeup. His "nurture" is his parenting and home and social environment. Which has the greater impact?

Why Is This Discussion Important?

Before the 1950's most people thought the mind of a newborn was a blank slate and that a child would behave as an angel if raised in the right environment. However, during the past few decades we have begun to realize the important role genetics, biological qualities, and general health contribute to behavior.

Parents of adopted children want to know how much their home environment matters when compared with the biological tendencies of their young child. Adoptive parents realize that their child brings with him certain physical characteristics, intellectual capabilities, personality traits, and disease tendencies and often wonder if these predetermined traits will inevitably get expressed regardless of the parenting they provide.

The Importance of the Nature of a Child

Deep inside our cells there is something programmed to come out: characteristics or diseases passed down from our past blood relatives to us. Human brain structures are very complex. More than 30,000 genes can influence our brain structure and function.

People who believe that a child's "nature" is the strongest influence in how a child turns out point to numerous research studies that show that a child's heredity affects most aspects of his behavior and mental health. These people will argue that identical twins separated at birth and raised in entirely different environments are often similar in their personality traits.

When the study of genetics first emerged, people wondered if science would find a gene for every aspect of our personalities (for instance, a "shy" gene). We now know that behavior is controlled by not one single identifiable gene, but by many.

The Importance of the Nurture of a Child

A large amount of research shows us that a child's social environment can increase the risk of aggression. Babies born with difficult deliveries or birth complications, who then experience maternal rejection, show an extremely high percent of violence as teens and adults.

Research has concluded that the following socioeconomic factors (nurture factors) can contribute significantly to a child's tendency to act out: poverty, parental illness or joblessness, hunger and nutritional deficiencies, homelessness, parental drug abuse, and domestic violence or instability. The incidence of behavioral disturbance in toddlers and preschoolers drops substantially when families find support to ameliorate the above socioeconomic stressors through assistance programs related to health care, food pantries, drug rehabilitation centers, and quality day care/preschool settings.

So What Is the Truth about This Debate?

The truth, as in most things in life, lands pretty close to the middle. Trying to define a child's behaviors strictly by her genetics or her environment is like trying to define a cube strictly by its height or width.

Six factors have an impact on a child's behaviors. Three of these factors are from the "nature" side (temperament, inherited vulnerability, and certain medical conditions) and three are from the "nurture" side (the quality of the parent-child attachment from birth, the presence, quality and timing of serious life stressors or attachment disruptions, and the type and quality of the home and parenting environment). How a child behaves, or his intelligence, or his amount of emotional self-control is based upon a complex interaction of many genetic variations coupled with many factors specific to his environment.

Both "nature" and "nurture" interact to form a child's personality and inner sense of who she is. Additionally, the developmental age of a child contributes to the relative importance of the nature versus nurture influences. For example, in the first three years, a child's personality is strongly molded by the interaction between her parents (or her primary caregiver) and her temperament. As she grows older, her biological temperament becomes less important. Instead, her environment (the impact of the people around her, the places she goes, the things she sees and learns, the stresses she experiences) interacts with her genetic vulnerabilities to play the largest part in determining her personality. Researchers are discovering that even when we have a genetic weakness (making us prone to a certain disease or characteristic), we still have a certain amount of influence on whether or not, and how strong this will appear. Our brains are also very plastic—biology can shape behavior and behavior can shape biology. Our brain's genetic structure as well as the environment our brain is exposed to throughout our life influence our personality. Research has demonstrated that huge stressors or depression can actually change the structure and function of our brains.

There are conditions that have a strong inherited basis and can play a strong role in a child's excessive behaviors (e.g., ADHD, certain types of depression and other mood disorders, Tourette's syndrome, autism, and a particular gene that increases the likelihood of serious antisocial behaviors). If a child is showing behavioral problems, it could be because of his genetic and inherited vulnerability. However, researchers admit that while infants may be born with certain genetic tendencies, the environment into which the child is born is still critical as to whether or not the child eventually develops the full-blown syndrome. Even if your child is genetically prone to a specific behavioral condition, it doesn't mean that he is doomed.

If your child has high-risk nature or nurture risk factors, there is no doubt that these will likely play a role in how she acts, but proper parenting can make the difference between health and illness. Regardless of how messed up your child's biology, heredity, genetics, health or home life is or has been, you still play a huge role on how your child turns out. Changing your parenting by following the Three Parenting Principles will change your life and the life of your tot or preschooler.

APPENDIX #2

The Eight Categories of Temperament

Have you noticed that biological brothers and sisters from the same family are often incredibly different? Even though parents often believe they have raised their children the same way, they are often astounded by how different each child is. Researchers in the past few decades have consistently identified inborn temperaments or traits that are individual to each person. The unique traits evident at birth can help us understand why siblings are often very different in their personalities. Some of these temperamental differences are more evident in certain children than others and in most children, some traits seem to be more dominant than the others are, even though all traits are present in all children to varying degrees and descriptions.

There are eight ways in which to categorize a child's temperamental traits:

#1. Activity

Glen's mother thinks of her four-year-old as "a constant motion machine." Glen's physical motion when he sleeps, plays, eats, bathes, and dresses is astounding. He virtually bounces and whirls from one activity to another. As an infant, he squirmed, bounced, and crawled excessively. Now as a preschooler, even when Glen watches TV, he taps his foot or wiggles in some way.

Four-year-old Rhonda is about as opposite of Glen as one can get. She is more like a tortoise than a hare; when her daddy arrives home she is happy to greet him, but she walks slowly to him while grinning widely. Rhonda's mom remembers the diapering phase as a time when her daughter usually lay quietly on the table, frequently content to gaze at her mobile.

You can place every child upon a scale from calm to excessively active. Where does your child fall?

#2. Predictability

Three-year-old Peter has always seemed to have a consistency about him. His mother remembers that he has always wanted to eat at regular times, and he falls asleep about the same time every night. His sleep requirements seem about the same every night and his bowels move regularly. Because his body functions are so predicable, Peter was easy to toilet train.

Loretta on the other hand seems to have no inner clock or interest in a set schedule. Since birth she has varied tremendously in her sleep and eating needs. As an infant, some days she seemed ravenous in her appetite, while the next day she would not be interested in drinking much at all. Now a preschooler, her bowels and sleep requirements continue to be unpredictable, which conflicts with her parents' interest in toilet training her as early as possible.

Where on this temperament scale does your child land?

#3. Adaptability

Lydia, a preschooler, seems to be unfazed when she experiences new people or new situations. When she is introduced to new foods, she tries them with gusto. When a new babysitter arrives, Lydia doesn't seem particularly ruffled and is happy and willing to show off her room. When plans change abruptly, Lydia is initially upset but is able to refocus her excitement about new plans.

Phil on the other hand has always seemed almost the opposite of Lydia. He is hesitant when faced with new situations. Even as a young tot he would pull back from new experiences and protest loudly to changes in his routine. As a preschooler Phil still seems to be quite upset when he faces new people, new places, and new foods. He will warm up slowly, but it takes him time. When plans change, Phil has a fit even if the new plans would likely be more exciting to him if those plans had been presented first.

How does your child compare to Lydia and Phil?

#4. Intensity

Since birth, Carla has expressed herself with high volume. She has always both laughed and cried loudly. As a preschooler now, she seems to love bright lights and lots of activity around her. Her mom always knows when Carla disapproves of something since the child always reacts with a raised voice.

Contrasting with Carla, Al since birth usually whimpers when upset instead of crying loudly. Al's mother notices that he has mild reactions to things like tickling or painful falls when compared to other kids she observes at the playground.

What is your child's overall intensity trait?

#5. Mood

Preschooler Larry has maintained a cheerful mood most of his life. He always seems to laugh, smile, or giggle a lot and seems to have a sunny upbeat personality.

Shirlee, on the other hand, has always seemed very serious and sometimes even glum. Her parents have always noticed that people frequently ask "is she a little sad or blue today?" even when her parents know that she is merely standing back and quietly observing the situation.

Does your child appear to have a predominantly upbeat or discerning disposition?

#6. Persistence

Preschooler Rosa seems to stick with one puzzle until she solves it. She has always had a long attention span and as an infant stared for several minutes at each of her hanging mobiles over her crib.

Young Curtis on the other hand didn't seem much interested in looking at the toys dangling around his stroller. Now as a preschooler, he doesn't seem to have the patience to sit very long if a task is frustrating to him. Trying to shoot the ball into the low basket his dad made for him doesn't keep his attention very long.

Is your child highly attentive and persistent, or does he seem unwilling to stay with the same activity very long?

#7. Distractibility

Edna as a baby was easily and quickly soothed when her mother walked out of the room. All anyone had to do was say something like, "Oh look here . . . look at this pretty flower" and she seemed to forget why she was crying. As she has entered her preschool years, she seems easily sidetracked by sirens and dogs barking even if she has been concentrating on drawing her picture.

Harvey, on the other hand, has always seemed difficult to distract if he wanted a certain toy or food. As a preschooler, he seems not to even notice the dog running in the yard when he plays with his truck.

Is your child easily distracted by stimuli he encounters or does he sometimes seem totally unperturbed by sights and sounds and keep doing what he was doing?

#8. Sensitivity

Kalee has always been sensitive to touch, hearing, and temperature. She has never been able to tolerate scratchy clothing. She holds her ears when near loud traffic and seems to be too hot or too cold when she is in the car. Kalee has a very narrow variety of tastes that she can stand and has always reacted with displeasure when her food is anything other than room temperature.

Peter, on the other hand, seems oblivious to temperatures and textures. He can easily play outside when it is freezing and he forgets his coat. He is happy to wear clothing of any fabric as long as he can get it dirty. In fact, he doesn't seem to react much to any of his five senses.

How strongly does your child react to smells, loud sounds, bright lights, texture, and temperature?

Many parents can describe their tot or preschooler as showing strong consistent responses to one or more of the above eight traits. If one or more traits seem to hold constant as your child develops, it is likely that this trait is something she was born with and will persist as she gets older. When a child's difficult behaviors are due to inborn biological characteristics you will often see these temperamental qualities "played out" differently depending upon the age.

Temperament sometimes heavily influences toddlers and preschoolers' difficult behaviors. If your child's frequent bouts of difficult and out-of-control behaviors are due in large part to his temperament, you will likely describe him in the following way: high activity, low body function predictability, low adaptability, high intensity, negative moods, low persistence, high distractibility, and high sensitivity. Clearly, the more this list matches your child's temperamental traits, potentially the more extreme your child's behaviors may be.

Ten Formal Mental Health Diagnoses That Can Have an Impact on a Child's Behavior

These ten basic areas of psychiatric disorders have been given a formal diagnosis as defined by the *Diagnostic and Statistical Manual of Mental Disorders IV.* This book is published by the American Psychiatric Association and is utilized by most clinicians who work in the mental health field of health care services. In general, the behavioral difficulties associated with each of the following ten mental health disorder categories have other symptoms associated with them not typically seen in children with normal developmental extreme behaviors. If you suspect your child may have one of these conditions, you should take him for a complete evaluation by his primary care or pediatric physician or nurse practitioner.

1. Attachment Disorders

Attachment disorders include separation anxiety disorder and re-active attachment disorder. Preschool children with separation anxiety disorder are excessively anxious (far more than expected for their developmental level) when separated from their home or from their parents or close family members. The disorder fre-quently develops after a significant life stress such as the death or serious illness of a close relative or pet or a move to a new home. The child may show signs of excessive worry, social withdrawal, deep sadness, or terrifying fears of animals, monsters, the dark, etc. Reactive attachment disorder (RAD—see also Appendix #5— Disorganized Attachment) typically begins before the age of five and usually occurs when the infant or child is exposed to early sep-arations from or changes in their primary caregiver or in cases where there is an extreme personality disconnect between the in-fant or young child and the parent. Children with RAD have markedly disturbed behaviors including not being affectionate on their parents' terms, showing intense displays of rage or mood swings particularly when given parental limits or controls, being superficially charming, bossy and controlling, and not wanting to make direct eye contact with their parents. Attachment disordered kids need to believe they are in control of things. They would of-ten rather take 10 hours to do something their way than 10 sec-onds of doing it their parents' way.

2. Attention Deficit and Disruptive Behavioral Disorders

ADHD is covered in Chapter 8. Kids are diagnosed with ADHD when they have serious persistent problems with attention, im-pulsivity, or hyperactivity. Children below age seven who are for-mally diagnosed with ADHD are usually described by their parents as having shown many of the following symptoms during toddler and preschool years: low frustration tolerance, frequent temper outbursts, bossiness, stubbornness, excessive and persistent insistence that their demands be met, serious mood swings, and extreme sensitivity to rejection from playmates.

The other major disruptive behavioral disorder seen in this category is Oppositional Defiant Disorder (ODD). Children with this disorder are often described as being constantly and continuously negativistic, defiant, disobedient, and hostile toward their parents. These kids argue constantly, resist parents' authority, and defy or refuse to comply with their parents' wishes while deliberately doing things they know will annoy them. They are often angry, blaming, vindictive, and spiteful in a way that significantly interferes with the normal functioning of the family. Their stubbornness and resistance to directions, unwillingness to compromise, and deliberate continual testing of limits often leaves their parents extremely annoyed and exhausted. As the ODD child nears the end of the preschool age, it is apparent that the child's behaviors are consistently bringing out the worst in both the parent and child. ODD often occurs along with the diagnosis of ADHD, bipolar disorder, or Reactive Attachment Disorder (RAD) and is frequently seen in kids whose parents rule with harshness, inconsistency, or severe punishments, or where the child's care has been disrupted by a series of caregivers (as seen in foster care and some adoption placements).

3. Communication Disorders

Children with communication disorders commonly have difficulty in their ability to communicate verbally or by sign language. Communication disorders are different from generalized developmental problems, mental retardation, hearing or motor deficits, or severe home deprivation problems. A young child with a communication disorder has a limited range or slow speed of speech, vocabulary, or word-finding ability, or a generalized slow rate of language or poor fluency or stuttering when compared to the vast majority of kids his age. A child might have this problem because of an earlier medical condition that affected his brain's language center (encephalitis or other brain infection, head trauma, or irradiation of the head to treat cancer). Children with this mental disorder often "act out" or withdraw from their playmates or family because of their anxiety, frustration, or insecure feelings about themselves.

4. Developmental Disorders

The behavioral symptoms of tots and preschoolers with Pervasive Developmental Disorders (PDD) include often extremely difficult and out-of-control behaviors such as severe tantrums, aggression, and self-injuring. This category includes the disorders of autism, Rett's Disorder, Childhood Disintegrative Disorder, and Asperger's Disorder. PDDs are characterized by severe and pervasive impairments in social interaction skills, communication skills, and/or the presence of an abnormally repetitive behavior, interest, or activity.

Autism appears to be strongly genetically predetermined since if a twin has autism there is almost a 90% chance that the identical twin, even when raised in a completely different home, will suffer from autism. The essential feature of autism is the presence before the age of three of an impaired development in social interaction and communication with a markedly restricted area of activity and interests. Autistic tots commonly do not look their parents in the eyes, do not seem interested in interacting or talking with family members, and seem oblivious to sharing facial expressions with people trying to communicate with them. They often have severe trouble in interacting with their peers and seem to have little or no interest in playing with other kids. Additionally, autistic tots and preschoolers are often preoccupied with one narrow interest or movement and they may launch into a rage to a touch or minor change in their surroundings. New research on autistic kids shows subtle brain abnormalities in infants and toddlers: their head circumference varies from most kids, starting too small and growing in spurts, parts of their brain have too many neural connections, and their brains show signs of chronic inflammation.

Children with Rett's Disorder (seen only in females and frequently associated with mental retardation) characteristically have a loss (between five to 40 months) of a previously normal head circumference; they wring their hands and have a very poorly coordinated gait.

In Childhood Disintegrative Disorder, there is normal development until the age of two to four years when the child disintegrates into the problems associated with autism. The behavioral symptoms that occur just prior to this severe decline in development include parent-perceived out-of-control behaviors like irritability and hyperactivity.

In Asperger's Disorder, the preschooler may have normal development and then begin to act uncoordinated or clumsy. After this, the young child begins a developmental decline of a markedly impaired ability to interact appropriately socially accompanied by repetitive behavioral movements or interests (similar to those seen in autism).

5. Feeding, Eating, or Elimination Disorders

These eating and elimination disorders are not the typical frustrations and hassles most parents experience in feeding and toilet training their kids; instead they are way outside of the normal deviations and are not associated with any medical conditions. The

disorders include such severe deviations as eating non-food substances like paint, dirt, animal droppings, and sand, a severe failure to eat adequately along with severe failure to gain weight, the
repeated passage of stool in inappropriate places after the age of
four, and the repeated passage of urine in inappropriate places after the age of five. Children with these conditions often act out
because of their feelings of severe stress as a reaction to their home
situation.

6. Learning Disorders

Preschoolers with learning disorders sometimes have an inability
to understand the information that is presented to them by their
preschool teachers. They may suffer from their visual, language,
attention, or memory deficits. Sometimes these deficits are a result of their medical conditions such as lead poisoning, exposure
to alcohol as a fetus, or a genetic condition called Fragile X Syndrome. While toddlers and preschoolers rarely receive the formal
diagnosis of learning disorder (because they have not entered formal schooling), preschooler teachers can observe early signs of
impending reading, mathematical, or writing difficulties. Children with signs of early learning disorders often feel badly about
themselves as they compare themselves to the achievements of
other preschoolers and respond to this by acting out.

7. Mental Retardation

The condition of Mental Retardation is one of the categories of
mental disorders commonly seen in children who have a diagnos-
able mental illness associated with out-of-control behaviors. Children who have mental retardation can have a severity that ranges
from mild to profound. The predominant symptom for children
with mental retardation is subnormal general intellectual func-

tioning evident in their general communication skills and their ability to provide themselves with self-care. Children with significant intellectual deficits can display severe behavioral problems due to their frustration about their limited ability to cope with some of the common life demands expected for their age group.

8. Mood Disorders

This category includes Depression Disorder and Bipolar Disorder (BD). Both Depression Disorder and Bipolar Disorder are two common psychiatric mood diagnoses with a strong component of "inherited vulnerability." Children whose parents have a history of a bipolar disorder, severe mood swings, serious depression, or a history of going for long periods without sleep are at particularly high risk.

Adult depressive disorders are characterized by having a depressed mood or having a loss of interest or pleasure in life (for more than two weeks) when accompanied by at least three of the following additional symptoms: significant weight or appetite loss or gain, difficulty sleeping, serious restlessness, serious fatigue, feelings of worthlessness or guilt, difficulty in concentrating or thinking, or recurrent thoughts of death or wanting to end one's life. Some families may be more vulnerable to depression than others due to biological differences in their brain hormones. In identical twin studies (when the twins are reared apart), there is up to a 40% chance that a second twin will have depression if the first one does. Crises and serious losses are often a trigger for a major depression for the parent as well as the child. Stressful events in the home can trigger a young child into depression in part because kids tend to "disasterize" their perspectives and thoughts about the life stress. Additionally, depression in a parent places a young child at risk because a depressed parent is less able to provide a secure attachment with the child (See Appendix #5).

The most significant difference between the symptoms of a young child with depression versus an adult is that instead of a deeply disabling sad mood and weight and energy changes, the child is more likely to have slowed growth and maturity and extreme irritability.

Adult bipolar disorders are characterized by having a manic episode(s) that may or may not be accompanied by depression at other times. During the manic episode, the person has an abnormally elevated or irritable mood for at least one week during which at least three of these other symptoms are present: an inflated sense of self, a decreased need for sleep where three hours "feels like enough," nonstop talkativeness, racing speech or having racing thoughts, extreme distractibility or inability to focus, an abnormal increase in activity or agitation, or excessive involvement in unwise pleasurable activities (daredevil actions, gambling, spending, sexual indiscretions, etc.). The most significant difference between early childhood and adult bipolar disorders is that frequently a young child's manic episode lasts shorter than one week or is accompanied by an extreme co-occurring irritability or depression.

9. Motor Skills Disorder

Young children with Motor Skills Disorder may display a level of clumsiness and serious developmental delay in achieving the normal motor milestones expected of their age group. For example, tots with this disorder may show an excessive developmentally slow ability to sit, crawl, walk, button or zip clothing, or tie shoelaces. Preschoolers may have profound problems in assembling puzzle pieces (even though they know where they want the piece to go), building blocks, or playing ball. In order to be given this diagnosis, the delay in motor skills development must not be associated with general medical conditions (such as cerebral palsy, stroke, abnormal nerve conditions, or muscular dystrophy). Behavioral problems in children with this disorder are commonly due to their extreme frustrations at not being able to do the things they see other kids doing that they know they have the mental capacity to perform.

10. Tic Disorders

Tic disorders tend to run in families, particularly through the males. Tic disorders include Tourette's syndrome, and chronic motor and vocal disorders. A tic is a sudden rapid recurrent intermittent and variable movement or vocalization usually brought on by stress. Tourette's syndrome is characterized by multiple motor tics and one or more verbal tics appearing at the same time or at different periods during the illness. The movements typically include touching, squatting, deep knee bends and twirling while the verbal tics include eye blinking, clicks, grunts, barks, snorts, and coughs. Kids with tic disorders often have more hyperactivity, impulsivity, and distractibility than is typical for their age. While the onset can begin as early as age two, the median age onset is age seven.

A Newly Emerging Diagnostic Category

While not listed in the *Diagnostic and Statistical Manual of Mental Disorders IV,* some researchers are interested in a relatively newly described sensory disorder frequently called a Sensory Processing Disorder (SPD). Some researchers and clinicians are convinced that children and adults with this condition have a disturbance in their capacity to interpret and subsequently act on the information they receive from their senses, thus creating difficulties in learning, functioning socially appropriately, or performing daily tasks. Many occupational therapists believe that they are the most qualified clinicians to help children with this condition. Because the knowledge status on SPD is still relatively new, substantial work and rigorous research must be done before many clinicians will diagnose and recommend a treatment intervention.

Medical Conditions Can Increase the Behavior Problems in Your Young Child

Serious illnesses in a child can have a strong negative impact on a toddler or preschooler's behaviors. If you suspect that your child may have any of the conditions listed below, be certain to visit your child's health care provider as soon as possible. The following list covers many of the most common medical and health problems that can have a large impact on your kid's behaviors:

❏ Premature birth causes immature brains with difficulty in calming self or controlling anger or irritability.

❏ Frequent ear infections or large tonsils can cause snoring and sleep disturbances.

❏ Poor nutrition or a high sugar diet can cause hyperactivity and/or irritability.

❏ Childhood onset diabetes can cause mood swings related to changes in blood sugar.

❏ Medications your child may be taking can cause irritability and anger.

❏ Asthma and its medications can cause irritability and hyper-activity.

❑ Allergies can sap a child's ability to stay calm due to cellular reaction to certain substances.

❑ Visual or hearing impairments can cause a child to act up to compensate.

❑ Endocrine disorders can cause too high or too low a thyroid hormone affecting sleep.

❑ Pain or fever from a broad variety of health problems can cause an increase in behavioral difficulties.

APPENDIX #4

Communication Phrases to Avoid

Sometimes parents unconsciously say things to their youngsters in ways that, if used consistently, contribute to a form of emotional, mental, or spiritual abuse or trauma to their child. Most parents use one or more of these communication behaviors at one or more times during their child's early childhood. If you find that you do this some of the time, do not worry. Most healthy parents resort to one or more of these occasionally, particularly during stressful times. The list is important to read, though, since you will want to assure yourself that the *vast majority* of your verbal communications with your child do *not* include the following phrases or messages:

❑ Insulting ("Can't you do anything right?" "I wish you were better.")

❑ Negative teasing ("How can someone so short reach that?" "What are you going to do about it, dummy?")

❑ Laughing at, joking about ("Why are you always so lame?" "Look how the little guy peed his pants.")

❑ Inflicting guilt ("Only a bad kid would think of that." "I've sacrificed my life for you.")

❑ Shaming, humiliating ("You are so worthless." "Shame on you!")

❑ Overpowering or bullying ("You tiny little man, you can't do anything right." "Just try to hit me again and I'll take you down.")

❑ Criticizing ("How can you be so stupid?" "Why are you always ruining things?")

❑ Degrading, disgracing ("What a pathetic attempt at crayoning this is." "No one will love you if you act like this.")

❑ Deceiving, tricking ("I never promised that"—*when you did promise it.* "I promise I'll give you this if you do that"—*when you have no intention of following through.* "That did not happen"—*when it did.*)

❑ Betraying ("Guess what he just said?" "You'll never believe what I just saw the kid doing.")

❑ Hurting, being cruel ("You've always been my troubled child." "I wish to God you were never born.")

❑ Intimidating, threatening ("I'm going to spank you within an inch of your life." "You do that again and you'll never see the light of day again.")

❑ Patronizing, condescending ("I'm always right and you are always wrong." "You'll never be able to do that as well as your sister.")

❑ Inflicting fear ("I'm going to leave you here." "I'll go away if you do that again.")

❑ Withdrawing/withholding love ("How could anyone love you when you do that?" "I could never love a kid who looks this dirty.")

❑ Raising hopes falsely (saying, "We'll see" or, "Maybe" repeatedly—*when you have no intention of ever doing it.*)

❑ Disallowing feelings ("You should (or shouldn't) feel . . ." "Big boys don't cry.")

❑ Stifling emotional expression ("You don't feel that way!" "It didn't really hurt.")

Why, you may ask, is it hard sometimes to avoid saying some of these phrases to your child during periods of intense stress? Unfortunately, young tots and preschoolers can serve as scapegoats for their parents. Young children often make perfect scapegoats because they exhibit all the vices that adults sometimes hold deep within them, don't want to admit about themselves, or hate about themselves (guilt, selfishness, sexual feelings, jealousy, tempers, stubbornness, greed, etc.). A parent who was himself traumatized in his own childhood, who has denied the pain from his early childhood conflicts (see Chapter 10), and who has emerged from his childhood with guilt about certain behaviors or failures is prone to become seriously and unreasonably intolerant of these qualities in his offspring. Such a parent attributes his own faults to his child. In other words, such a parent is apt to torment his child with verbal insults in a vain attempt to rid the child of the qualities that he hates within himself.

Behavior Connected with Attachment Quality

Virtually all children attach to their primary caregiver, though the *quality* of their attachment varies. The "attachment quality" a child has with his mother and/or father depends upon two main influences:

❑ The quality of the interaction between the parent and the child affected by the sensitivity and adaptation of the parent to the child's innate temperament (see Appendix #2).

❑ The child's inherent reaction to and interpretation of his parent and environment (also affected by the child's temperament).

Early attachment relationships actually influence a young child's brain development, which can result in lasting influences at a brain structure and function level. Over time, the repetition of soothing eye contact, touch, and comfort allow brain pathways to become well developed with soothing patterned brain structures so that the child becomes biologically able to soothe and regulate her own upset emotions. Lack of soothing eye contact, touch, and comfort in infancy and early childhood can cause brain pathways to under-develop in ways that are important for mental health, thus placing the child at risk for mental illness and chronic psychiatric problems.

Early attachment relationships also serve as a foundation for an infant, toddler, and preschooler to learn how to control his moods. For example, when a mother comforts her young child's distress, the child begins to learn how to regulate his own self-upsets. Through observing and interacting with an attachment figure, a child learns what it is like to behave and have influence in a relationship.

The attachment relationship also serves as an expected model of how the infant and young child imagines and anticipates the future world will treat her. An infant who is treated sensitively grows to see the world as generally good and herself as deserving of being treated well. An infant, toddler, or preschooler who is treated harshly, erratically, or not at all grows to see the world as unpredictable and insensitive and views herself as not deserving any better treatment than what she has already received.

Insecure attachment relationships do not *cause* future problems. Rather they initiate probable pathways. How a child/adolescent/adult turns out is always the joint result of two factors: his early history and his ongoing environmental circumstances. When a child views himself in a certain way based upon how he perceived the attachment relationship, he tends to use these thoughts about himself as a model of expectations and beliefs about himself, other people, and relationships. These thoughts extend into his teen and adult years. When a child feels a certain way deep down about himself, he tends to interpret, select, and influence the people and circumstances around him in a way that keeps his behavior and his brain neuronal connection pathways consistent to the way he felt as a child. Therefore, an insecurely attached child is at much higher risk for future problems.

Research is abundant with evidence that infants and young children who are insecurely attached show much higher levels of anger, sadness, and aggression as they grow up. For example, securely attached children develop abilities for self-control and knowledge on how to behave in response to the wishes of another person. Insecurely attached two-year-olds are less able to tolerate frustrations. Insecurely attached preschoolers are more socially withdrawn, less likely to show sympathy for injured or unhappy playmates, are less willing to interact with friendly adults, and are more likely to display aggression and disobedience.

What follows is a presentation of a young child and the typical behavior signs seen in children with each type of attachment:

Jason—A Typical Child with a Secure Attachment

Jason's mother spent a lot of time with him during his infancy and first few years and was highly attuned to his personality. Though Jason as an infant was quite fussy, his mom rocked and held him close to her and was soothingly quiet during his fussy times until he settled down in exhausted slumber. She discovered unique and specific ways to hold him, feed him, carry him, and put him to sleep that seemed to keep him calmer. As a toddler his behavior while shopping often became extremely difficult. During his tantrums, his mom carried him outside to the car and calmly waited until his fits subsided. After the tantrum she would explain why he couldn't have what he demanded. She usually talked directly into his eyes while holding him on her lap or gently holding his hands. If he began to wail again she would patiently wait until he quieted down before talking to him about the behaviors she expected of him while in the store. Soon she found she could predictably anticipate his difficult behaviors, so she made plans that would allow her to avoid being terribly frazzled by him.

Jason believed to his core that his mom was available, responsive, and dependable. He didn't experience much fear since he knew he could depend upon his mom to be there for him. As a toddler and preschooler, Jason used his mom as a secure base from which he could explore his environment. He learned that his mom did not like it when he acted out-of-control but that she would remain near him until he "got a grip." He became more and more able to control his own angry or sad emotions. As a preschooler, Jason felt more and more competent in his ability to be around other people, always knowing he could depend on his mom to protect him or give him reassurance.

Typical Behaviors Seen with a Secure Attachment

Securely attached infants, toddlers, and preschoolers still show fear, sadness, anger, or anxiety at times—these are normal human reactions. But these young children are able to rely on their caregivers for comfort and protection if necessary. Securely attached infants, toddlers, and preschoolers feel comforted by their primary caregivers when they feel threatened. They are able to explore their world because they have confidence that their caregiver will help them if they have trouble. Because they are confident in the sensitive and responsive availability of their caregivers they are confident in themselves.

Christine—A Typical Child with an Anxious Attachment

Christine as an infant found her father (her sole attachment figure because of an absentee mother) to be incredibly nervous and uncertain about how to care for her. He was tentative about holding or rocking her, and often left her for quite long periods in her infant swing, car seat, and carrier. Christine hated being left alone and would scream for attention. Sometimes her dad would run quickly to her aid, but even then, it seemed that he was too busy and preoccupied with his friends and their conversations to spend much time holding her or talking to her directly. Often when he would feed her, he would not look in her eyes or even in her direction—while Christine sat in her carrier he would hold the bottle for her in one hand and talk on his cell phone with the other. Sometimes when Christine cried, no one would come to check on her for many minutes. When her father did come to her aid, he was often eager to leave her side as soon as she was soothed. Christine began clinging desperately to him when he held her, because she didn't want to be left alone. But Christine's demanding and clinging behavior really bugged her dad who started making more excuses not to be around her.

As a toddler, Christine would wail when her dad left her sight because she couldn't depend upon when he would come back. Christine's dad would sometimes sneak away when she wasn't expecting it just so he could avoid hearing her wails of protest. Each time he left her, Christine felt abandoned and desperately needed his attention and presence. When he returned, Christine often became overcome with anger and rage; in the midst of this anger, she would swing at him, which just made him less interested in being with her. Christine became very guarded and cautious because she never really knew what to expect from her dad. Sometimes she felt like she could cope with the world when she was holding on to his legs for security. But she feared other people and the world when Dad wasn't right by her side. She doubted her own ability to do anything.

As a preschooler, Christine didn't feel good about herself. She became chronically dependent upon others for immediate support and affirmation. She was particularly vulnerable to stress (she suffered from stomachaches, headaches, or wheezing when the family tensions were high) and she felt helpless and very sad or angry a lot of the time. It seemed to her that almost every friendship she made was filled with disappointments. She absolutely hated being alone without comfort or protection and lived in almost constant fear of things such as the dark, spiders, monsters, and thunder.

Typical Behaviors Seen with an Anxious Attachment

Anxiously attached infants, toddlers, and preschoolers have not experienced consistent availability of and comfort from their caregivers when their environment has proven threatening. Their requests for attention are often met with rebuff, indifference, or with inconsistent comfort. They become anxious about the availability of their caregiver, fearing that the caregiver will be unresponsive or ineffectively responsive when needed. They often show anger toward their caregiver for their lack of responsiveness and perhaps as a way to punish their caregiver in the hope that their caregiver will become more consistently available. Anxiously attached infants, toddlers, and preschoolers do not feel free to explore their environment without worry, so they cannot achieve the same mastery and confidence in themselves as securely attached children.

Brittany—a Typical Child with an Avoidant Attachment

Soon after Brittany's birth, the family experienced a tragedy with her sibling—Brittany's brother was injured in a freak accident in their backyard. For many months, Brittany's mother was not emotionally available to care for her. When Brittany cried, her mom would rush to her side as if she was on fire. Her sudden appearance looming over the crib scared Brittany. As soon as her mother determined that Brittany was not choking, she would frantically try to calm her. When this didn't work, she would become frustrated and just walk away. Often when Brittany crawled over to her mom and raised her hands to be held and protected, her mom would either coldly and stiffly pick her up, or make fun of her request to be held or hugged. When Brittany would pout or whimper with sadness, her mom would command her to "stop your whining."

When Brittany was a toddler, rare was the time when the two of them melted into each other's arms, even when they were laughing. Brittany soon found that she could not depend upon her mother to reassure or nurture her, so she discovered ways to soothe herself. Rocking back and forth on her knees and arms and constant finger sucking really helped her to feel better. Every day she found new ways to take care of her own needs. Soon she stopped asking for protection, reassurance, or comfort from anyone in her life (including her mom, dad, or babysitter). Brittany's mom described her as an impressively self-sufficient toddler who didn't seem to want much from her parents. Brittany's mom viewed this as a blessing since she was preoccupied caring for her handicapped son. Sometimes Brittany's mom secretly admitted to herself that she was so emotionally exhausted that she just didn't have an ounce of comfort left for anyone.

As a preschooler, Brittany believed deep down that she couldn't trust others to give her support or attention. She realized that she needed to live her life on her own terms. She soon found ways to manipulate her mom into giving her almost whatever she wanted. She discovered that her mom feared her tantrums so much that Brittany "called all the shots" in the house. Brittany gave little care about the feelings of her parents or others. Things needed to go her way or she would see to it that people regretted it.

Typical Behaviors Seen with an Avoidant Attachment

Avoidant attached infants, toddlers, and preschoolers perceive their primary caregivers as completely insensitive to them and dislike or want to avoid contact with them. These young children avoid, downplay, or deny their needs for comfort and protection—they are often described by others as "a loner" or "very self-reliant" even at a young age. In the presence of their primary caregiver, they commonly display one or more of the signs and symptoms of grief normally experienced by infants, toddlers, and preschoolers who face a total loss and absence of their mothers (protest, anger, despair, and detachment).

Sam—A Typical Child with a Disorganized Attachment

Before birth, Sam was exposed to smoking and occasional crack cocaine. When Sam was born, chaos reigned in his parents' lives. Both his parents drank excessively. Some days they would leave him all night to go to a nightclub. He would be stuck in his crib with no one but his four-year-old sister to throw the bottle into the crib. When his parents were around, they would fight horribly, often throwing things against the wall. Sam would cower in fear under his covers, hoping their wrath would not fall on him again. Sometimes when he cried from hunger or fright, one of his parents would hit or shake him to "shut up"!

Sam became a "tough" little toddler. Sometimes he would scrap and fight ferociously with his sister. Other times he acted out his intense anger by trying to hurt the family pet. When his father yelled at him to stop throwing food, Sam would stubbornly stamp off to write all over the walls with a Magic Marker. Sometimes he would act like a caretaker for his parents by bringing them snacks and their slippers. When around strangers or neighbors who did not press him into relating, he would act engagingly charming.

As a preschooler, he became a "control freak" about his stuffed animal collection. If anyone messed the arrangement he had on his bed, he would fly into a rage and chase the perpetrator with a knife. He believed he had to take charge of everything or die. Deep down, Sam hated himself and every adult and playmate he met. Though Sam preferred to be alone, he had to be in charge if any other preschooler played with him. He would frequently hit, bite, scream, or stamp off in a fury, and he expressed anger if anyone tried to hug, hold, or talk kindly to him.

Typical Behaviors Seen with a Disorganized Attachment

Infants, toddlers, and preschoolers with a disorganized attachment perceive their primary caregivers as terribly frightening, abusive, or unavailable. They often become incoherently angry and controlling in their relationships with others. Though deep down they long for affection, they outwardly act removed, distant, distrustful and may become intensely anxious, depressed, or hostile if they are pushed into relating with someone else who shows kindness, warmth or tries close physical contact. These children are often superficially engaging and charming, lack impulse control, are destructive, exploitative, manipulative and chronically angry, are not affectionate on their parents' terms, cannot tolerate external limits or control, trust no one, and often lack remorse and empathy. They are often diagnosed with Reactive Attachment Disorder.

APPENDIX #6

When Should You Seek Help for Your Child and What Resources Are Available to You?

Signs of Abnormalities in a Tot or Preschooler That Warrant a Second Look

If a parent, close family member, preschool teacher, or respected outsider believes that a child may be acting "outside the norm," you should consider one of the following possible reasons for such a belief:

❏ The opinion may be wrong because of a lack of context, accurate information, or long enough exposure to evaluate properly.

❏ Your child may have a physical problem (mental retardation, serious chronic illness) that is having a strong impact on his behaviors.

❑ Your child may be exhibiting symptoms of a behavioral problem that should be fully evaluated by health care professionals.

Signs of mental health or emotional problems in tots or preschoolers often present themselves as physical symptoms (headache, stomachache, vague pain, etc.) or as a constellation of behavioral complaints covered in Chapters 3, 5, and 7. A genuinely emotionally disturbed child usually displays his symptoms in more than one environment (home, preschool, church, neighborhood, family gatherings, etc.).

Nonetheless, there are red flags that warrant evaluation by your child's Primary Care Provider. Read over the list below—if you answer all the questions with "yes" (up to your child's current age), you can be reasonably assured that your child is not showing signs or symptoms that warrant an immediate workup, evaluation, and intervention.

BY 12 MONTHS OF AGE:

❑ Does your child have and enjoy eye contact when you are rocking and cooing with her?

❑ Are you convinced that your child hears well?

❑ Does your child follow a progressive pattern of increasing communication (every month she is relating more than the previous month) to you and close family members beginning at age four months (smiling and showing interest in faces, etc.) to 12 months (playing peek-a-boo and other social playtime games and making early sounds like "ma," "ga," "da," etc.)?

BY 15–18 MONTHS OF AGE:

❑ Is your child capable of following simple instructions (jump, stop, no, etc.)?

❑ Does your child continue to improve each month in his ability to communicate, to demonstrate that he is learning about his environment (by pointing and uttering consistent sounds that mean something to both of you), and in his ability to point out known items and body parts ("show me your nose," etc.).

❑ Does your child learn a few new words each month so by age 18 months he understands and uses at least 10 words?

❑ Does your child continue to enjoy pleasing you and looking directly and lovingly in your eyes when you hold him during snuggle times?

❑ Is your child attempting to walk or does your child walk without falling frequently?

BY AGE 2:

❑ Does your child have a good sleep schedule and is she able to put herself back to sleep if she awakens at night?

❑ Does your child separate from you some of the time to explore her world?

❑ Does your child continue to appear smarter every month in the way she interacts with her world?

❑ Does your child understand at least 50 words, use at least two words together accurately ("big ball"), and is she able to name body parts and five pictures?

❑ Does your child enjoy eye contact, cuddling, and interacting with you and enjoy playing cooperatively with other young children?

❑ Can your child scribble on paper and walk downstairs using a rail?

BY AGE 3:

❏ Does your child seem happy and calm most of the time during the day?

❏ Does your child enjoy playing interactive games (including talking and taking turns) with other young children and close family members?

❏ Does your child play with you and playmates without biting, hitting, or kicking?

❏ Does your child string at least four clear words together that make sense ("Me go play park" "Baby cry want bottle")?

❏ Is your child able to answer who, what, where questions clearly?

❏ Can your child balance for one second on one foot, kick a ball, and jump with both feet together?

❏ Can your child hold and use a crayon without using his fist and copy a circle?

BY AGE 4:

❏ Does your child seem happy and calm most of the time during the day?

❏ Does your child follow game rules and follow limits and directions at home?

❏ Is your child fully toilet trained (except perhaps occasional night wetting)?

❏ Does your child always act kind and loving to pets, have no interest in fire starting, no intent to destroy objects or himself, and show no signs of sexual precociousness?

❏ Can your child separate relatively easily from you prior to brief planned explained absences?

❏ Is your child able to count to four and able to show you good judgment when she tells you what to do in case of danger, fire, or an interaction with a stranger?

❏ Can your child balance on one foot for four seconds and alternate steps when climbing stairs?

❏ Is your child able to feed herself and button her clothing?

❏ Is your child's speech clear to people outside the family?

BY AGE 5:

❏ Does your child seem happy and calm most of the time during the day?

❏ Does your child usually sleep peacefully at night?

❏ Can your child make and keep friends?

❏ Is your child able to dress himself (except tying his shoelaces)?

❏ Can you say you would *not* describe your child as any of the following: a bully, aggressive, frequently bullied, sexually precocious, cruel to animals, a loner, a firestarter?

❏ Is your child's speech 100% understandable and is he able to identify coins and six colors correctly?

❏ Can your child follow a three-step command ("lift up this sock, carry it to the couch, and then return to me")?

❏ Can your child copy a triangle and draw a person?

❏ Can your child hop and jump?

Great Sources of Help for Young Children

Stepfamily Association of America
http://www.saafamilies.org

Center for Mental Health Services
Substance Abuse and Mental Health
  Services Administration
Rm 12-105 Parklawn Building
Rockville, MD 20857
Phone: 301-443-8956
Fax: 301-443-9050
http://www.samhsa.gov

ERIC Clearinghouse on Disabilities
  and Gifted Education
1110 North Glebe Road
Arlington, VA 22201-5704
800-328-0272
E-mail: *ericec@cec.sped.org*
http://www.eric.ed.gov

National Institute of Mental Health
Office of Communications
6001 Executive Boulevard, Room 8184,
  MSC 9663
Bethesda, MD 20892-9663
Phone: 301-443-4513
Fax: 301-443-4279
Toll Free: 1-866-615-NIMH (6464)
E-mail: *nimhinfo@nih.gov*
http://www.nimh.nih.gov

American Academy of Child and
  Adolescent Psychiatry (AACAP)
3615 Wisconsin Avenue, NW
Washington, DC 20016-3007
Phone: 202-966-7300
Fax: 202-966-2891
http://www.aacap.org/index.htm

American Psychological Association
750 1st Street, NE
Washington, DC 20002-4242
Phone: 202-336-5510
Toll Free: 1-800-374-2721
http://www.apa.org

Child and Adolescent Bipolar
  Foundation
1187 Wilmette Avenue
PMB 331

Wilmette, IL 60091
Phone: 847-256-8525
Fax: 847-920-9498
http://www.bpkids.org

Department of Education Office of
  Special Education Programs
400 Maryland Ave, SW
Washington, DC 20202
Phone: 202-205-5465
*http://www.ed.gov/about/offices/list/osers/
  osep/index.html?exp=0*

Depression and Bipolar Support
  Alliance (DBSA)
730 N. Franklin Street, Suite 501
Chicago, IL 60610-7224
Phone: 312-642-0049
Fax: 312-642-7243
http://www.DBSAlliance.org

Federation of Families for Children's
  Mental Health
1101 King Street, Suite 420
Alexandria, VA 22314
Phone: 703-684-7710
Fax: 703-836-1040
E-mail: *ffcmh@ffcmh.org*
http://www.ffcmh.org

National Information Center for
  Children and Youth with Disabilities
  (NICHCY)
PO Box 1492
Washington, DC 20013
Fax: 202-884-8441
Toll Free: 800-695-0285
E-mail: *nichcy@aed.org*
http://www.nichcy.org

First Signs promotes early detection
  of Developmental and Behavioral
  Disorders.
First Signs, Inc.
P.O. Box 358
Merrimac, MA 01860
Phone: 978-346-4380
http://www.firstsigns.org
info@firstsigns.org

The Father's Network offers resources and support for families raising children with developmental disabilities and special health care needs.
Washington State Fathers Network
Kindering Center
16120 N.E. Eighth Street
Bellevue, WA 98008
425-747-4004
http://www.fathersnetwork.org

The Department of Health and Human Services has developed "a special initiative to support and strengthen the roles of fathers in families."
http://fatherhood.hhs.gov/index.shtml

The Children's Defense Fund states its mission is, "To ensure every child a Healthy Start, a Head Start, a Fair Start, a Safe Start, and a Moral Start in life."
http://www.childrensdefense.org

Family Voices is a "national, grassroots clearinghouse for information and education concerning the health care of children with special health needs."
http://www.familyvoices.org

The National Partnership for Women & Families is a "nonprofit, nonpartisan organization that uses public education and advocacy to promote fairness in the workplace, quality health care, and policies that help women and men meet the dual demands of work and family."
http://www.nationalpartnership.org

Strong Fathers—Strong Families is a training organization focused on helping children by strengthening their relationship with their fathers and families.
http://www.strongfathers.com

The Technical Assistance Alliance for Parent Centers "supports a unified technical assistance system for the purpose of developing, assisting and coordinating Parent Training and Information Projects and Community Parent Resource Centers under the Individuals with Disabilities Education Act (IDEA)."
http://www.taalliance.org

The Arc is the national organization of and for people with mental retardation and related developmental disabilities and their families.
http://www.thearc.org

The AARP helps educate its members about being grandparents.
http://www.aarp.org/life/grandparents

Casey Family Programs' mission is, "To provide and improve—and ultimately to prevent the need for—foster care."
http://www.casey.org

The Child Welfare League of America is, "The nation's oldest and largest membership-based child welfare organization committed to promoting the well-being of children, youth, and their families, and protecting every child from harm." *http://www.cwla.org*

Generations United is, "The only national membership organization focused solely on promoting intergenerational strategies, programs, and public policies. The organization advocates for the mutual well-being of children, youth, and older adults." *http://www.gu.org*

Index